IÑUPIAT OF THE SII

Iñupiat of the Sii

Historical Ethnography and Arctic Challenges

Wanni W. Anderson and Douglas D. Anderson

UNIVERSITY OF ALASKA PRESS
Fairbanks

© 2024 by University Press of Colorado

Published by University of Alaska Press
An imprint of University Press of Colorado
1580 North Logan Street, Suite 660
PMB 39883
Denver, Colorado 80203-1942

ASSOCIATION of UNIVERSITY PRESSES   The University Press of Colorado is a proud member of
the Association of University Presses.

The University Press of Colorado is a cooperative publishing enterprise supported, in part, by Adams
State University, Colorado State University, Fort Lewis College, Metropolitan State University of
Denver, University of Alaska Fairbanks, University of Colorado, University of Denver, University
of Northern Colorado, University of Wyoming, Utah State University, and Western Colorado
University.

∞ This paper meets the requirements of the ANSI/NISO Z39.48-1992 (Permanence of Paper).

ISBN: 978-1-64642-604-1 (hardcover)
ISBN: 978-1-64642-605-8 (paperback)
ISBN: 978-1-64642-606-5 (ebook)
https://doi.org/10.5876/9781646426065

Library of Congress Cataloging-in-Publication Data

Names: Anderson, Wanni W. (Wanni Wibulswasdi), 1937– author. | Anderson, Douglas D., author.
Title: Iñupiat of the Sii : historical ethnography and Arctic challenges / Wanni W. Anderson and
    Douglas D. Anderson.
Other titles: Historical ethnography and the Arctic challenges
Description: Fairbanks : University of Alaska Press, [2024] | Includes bibliographical references and
    index.
Identifiers: LCCN 2024002495 (print) | LCCN 2024002496 (ebook) | ISBN 9781646426041
    (hardcover) | ISBN 9781646426058 (paperback) | ISBN 9781646426065 (ebook)
Subjects: LCSH: Inupiat—Native Village of Selawik—Social life and customs. | Inupiat—Native
    Village of Selawik—History. | Native Village of Selawik—Social life and customs. | Native Village
    of Selawik—History. | Excavations (Archaeology)—Native Village of Selawik. | Anderson, Wanni
    W. (Wanni Wibulswasdi), 1937– | Anderson, Douglas D.
Classification: LCC E99.E7 A632 2024 (print) | LCC E99.E7 (ebook) | DDC
    979.8/6050049712—dc23/eng/20240220
LC record available at https://lccn.loc.gov/2024002495
LC ebook record available at https://lccn.loc.gov/2024002496

Cover art: plaque made by Leo Berry.

In memory of Nora Paaniikaaluk Norton, superb storyteller;
Emma Sailaq Norton, our first and best friend in Selawik;
Arthur Iquq Skin, who took Douglas hunting and kept watch over us;
and Ruthie Tatqaviñ Sampson, the book as promised.

Contents

Illustrations

TABLES

Prologue

Riverine Village by the Sii

There is no knowing or sensing the place except by being in that place, and to be in a place is to be in a position to perceive it. . . . Such knowledge, genuinely local knowledge, is itself experiential in the manner of Erlebnis, "lived experience."
—EDWARD S. CASEY (1996:18)

"Airplane!" a boy shouted excitedly.

The buzz of a small plane called the "siulik" by the Iñupiat for its sharp nose, reminiscent of a pike, flying close to the rooftops was loud. Many people rushed out of their homes, jumped into their outboard motorboats, and raced to be the first to arrive at the airport on the Siktaavik side of the Selawik River. Three times a week, incoming flights provided much village excitement. Some villagers boated to meet the plane to pick up their incoming friend or family member. Owners of the two village stores arrived in big boats to pick up their merchandise. The postmaster picked up the village mail. The custodian of the village school picked up the school mail and supplies. Others came to the airport just to see who came in and who went out. Some showed up at the dirt-packed airport just to see what type of goods arrived for their purchase. The box that held the most inquisitive, joking interest was merchandise that came in a liquor store box. "I wonder if there is a bottle in it?" Selawik was legally a dry village.

On Sunday, July 1, 1968, we were the two new faces that showed up at Selawik airport on a charter flight.

https://doi.org/10.5876/9781646426065.c000

We were members of the Brown University Archaeological Expedition, excavating since 1964 on the Kobuk River at Onion Portage, ten miles below Ambler village. The archaeology had attracted many local visitors, who wanted to see and learn what we were finding, since this was part of their cultural heritage. In August 1967, a surprise visitor arrived at Onion Portage on a small private plane. He introduced himself as the pastor of the Seventh-day Adventist Church on the Selawik, the river immediately south of the Kobuk River. John Topcock was a native Iñupiaq pastor, soft-spoken, and easy to talk to. He brought in a tape of gospel songs he had recorded at church meetings in Kotzebue, Shungnak, and Noorvik villages. He played the songs for all of us to hear. Later, when he heard that Doug, who had visited many villages in Northwest Alaska, had never visited Selawik, he invited us to visit. "It's a very nice village. People live on both sides of the Selawik River and on the island in the middle." That was indeed a different setting from the villages we were familiar with on the Kobuk, all situated on one bank of the river.

Douglas was fascinated. No ethnographer or archaeologist had ever studied this riverine village in a low-lying tundra landscape. Having an invitation from someone in the village who could vouch for us was a wise field research strategy since it conformed to the local code of conduct for visitors. Douglas, director of the Brown University Archaeological Expedition, temporarily assigned the excavation's supervision to a graduate archaeology student, then took a ten-day trip to explore Selawik. Wanni came with him with an assigned task. While Douglas explored for archaeological sites, Wanni, an anthropologist and folklorist, stayed in the village "to get to know the people," as Douglas put it, and see what Selawik was like culturally.

With Pastor Topcock's assistance, we were able to rent a house in the middle of the village, on Akuliġaq Island, not far from the Quaker Friends Church. Its owner, James Wells, was with his family at their summer fish camp downriver.

Next door to the Wells' house, a group of men were busy helping Pastor Walton of the Friends Church build his new house, a log cabin. We introduced ourselves to the group, and when they broke for lunch, the pastor invited us to join them. We filled them in further on why we were in Selawik. The people were friendly and warm. Then and there, we fulfilled the Iñupiaq time-honored code of conduct of newcomers informing the residents of the purpose of their visit.

The next day we walked around, exploring the village. From the Selawik riverbank, we saw the row of houses on the other side of the river. An eight- or nine-year-old boy whisked by on an outboard motorboat, all by himself. We hitched a ride across the river on a rowboat with an eight-year-old girl to see the village on "the school side of the river." The girl rowed surprisingly well for her young age. We walked around, and Douglas checked to see if anyone would be willing to boat him up the river for an archaeological survey. At the upper end of the village, we met Paul Ballot sitting in front of his house. Douglas managed to get a day trip to Sauniqtuuq the next day with Paul to see the old homestead of Qayaqtauginnaqtuaq, the Selawik/Iñupiaq legendary epic hero about whom we had heard so much (W. Anderson 2005).

Early the following morning, Johnny Foster, one of the men Doug had talked to the day before, showed up and said he would be glad to take Douglas on his survey. They shopped for food at the Rotman's village store and left the village a few hours later for their six-day trip upriver. Wanni, left behind by herself, a new face in a new village, braced herself for the anthropological "get to know the people."

Wanni introduced herself to more people, happily accepting invitations to go inside the house for visits with the families she met. Curious children showed up at her rented house to get to know her, and from them Wanni tried to learn about schooling and children's life. Her Asian face was a point of interest. "Which village did you come from?" a young man asked. A Buddhist who had been educated in a private Catholic girls' school, Wanni attended the service of the California Quaker Friends Church the following Sunday as a gesture of respect to the major faith of the people and to learn about the village church service. A few days later, a child passed away in a house not too far from where Wanni was staying, and she witnessed the child's funeral. She took photographs of the village, of her neighbor cutting fish to be dried. She met Emma Norton, who would become our best friend and mentor. From two elders, premier Selawik storytellers, Nora Norton and John Brown (W. Anderson 2005; Anderson and Sampson 2003), she was able to record during this short two-week stay her first set of thirteen stories and two songs from Selawik. Two days before our departure, we were treated to a fresh caribou steak dinner that James Wells brought back from his hunt at the summer camp. He graciously declined to accept our house rent.

Our first visit to Selawik and the welcoming reception of the Selawikers convinced us that Selawik was the right place to experience living and learning the whole-year life cycle of the Iñupiat. We hoped that would assist us in understanding Iñupiaq culture more fully than what we had learned from books and from excavating during the summers at Onion Portage.

There was no house for us to live in or to rent for the whole year. Our plan was to build our own house there, starting with requesting permission to reside in the village, and getting help from some village elders to find a suitable location for it. Since the core of the Iñupiaq existence is self-reliance, doing everything oneself even if one had never done it before, we were too embarrassed to contract a house to be built for us. We had no wish to appear helpless even before we started to live there. Bill Coperthwaite, a graduate student at Harvard University, heard about our project and our need. He wanted to experience Alaskan village life and volunteered to help us build a one-room wooden yurt that he had designed after the canvas Mongolian yurt. It would be a modest living accommodation, but it suited our purpose.

There was no lumber store in Selawik, so in August 1969, the three of us arrived in Selawik with the needed building materials precut and flown in from Anchorage. Douglas graduated from building a matchbox in grade school, and Wanni learned how to drive in nails, waterproof the roof, and stain and varnish the inside of the house. We finally had the beginnings of the house. It sat on the side of the Nigraq, a small channel that ran into the Selawik River. The house's location was selected by Roy Smith and David Greist, members of Selawik City Council, who welcomed our intended stay. Later on, we learned from a folktale that our allocated house site conformed to the Iñupiaq cultural pattern of newcomers living at the far side of village.

We stayed for two months, built the yurt, reconnected with those we had met the year before, and informed them of our planned longer stay in the village. The next summer, of 1971, Douglas returned to Selawik to finish building our house and to start the first thrust of our study, collecting information about the early history of the village.

Douglas received a leave of absence from teaching for the 1971–1972 academic year at Brown University, and Wanni shelved the completion of her doctoral dissertation at the University of Pennsylvania. In September, we returned to Selawik for our full-year stay, funded by Douglas's postdoctoral research fellowship from the Wenner-Gren Foundation. Our first priority was to winterize our house and make it more livable. We put in more finishing touches to our living space, building seats, storage spaces, and a cooking counter, and adding an outer ring to the yurt to further insulate the living room and create additional cold storage space. We acquired an Alouette snowmobile from the Blankenship Trading Post in Kiana to facilitate our winter travel within and outside the village. Snowmobiles were the current winter travel vehicle for villagers, having replaced dog teams during the previous decade. On our first ride, we felt we were moving closer to living the Iñupiaq way.

The year 1971–1972 was amazing and challenging. We learned how to live simply and to watch out for the unexpected to stay out of danger. Having two greenhorns experiencing the tough, below-zero Arctic winter for the first time among them, Selawikers were very generous, giving us helpful advice and keeping a watchful eye on our safety. We learned so much from everyone and learned to do new things we had never dreamed of doing. We made mistakes. We learned about our limitations but also new territories we could—and had to—cross if we were to live there. Wanni learned how to row, lived with melted snow and melted ice in a bucket for water, did the laundry Iñupiaq style, and enjoyed flying on the back of the sled runners, pulled by the snowmobile. Doug learned how to build his own boat and sled, and how to hunt for caribou for fresh meat. We felt richer for the gift of knowledge

Figure 0.1. Andersons' house on the Nigraq.

shared and the friendships given. We participated in community activities. Doug helped to dig a grave through the winter permafrost and assisted the search-and-rescue organization in staking a winter trail and refurbishing the shelter cabin between Selawik and Noorvik. Both of us helped substitute teach at the school. Wanni became an Arctic sunset freak and took myriad photographs of the magnificent sunsets behind an abandoned Ferguson mink farm across the river from where we lived. Aurora borealis flashed its spell-binding, colorful lights on some winter nights to delight our eyes and to remind us that we were indeed living far up in the Arctic.

Several years later, in 1976, Selawik, now a first-class city, sponsored an archaeological field school to acquaint students with their own Native heritage. The field school that Douglas conducted lasted for two weeks in August. Eight students participated in the excavation of an old settlement site at Fox River in the lake area west of Selawik.

The following year, we made a short stay from June 2 to July 20, 1977. This gave Douglas further opportunities to survey more Selawik archaeological site locations and allowed Wanni to reconnect with Selawik friends and learn more about Selawik folklore and summer lifeways. It also provided her with the time and access to records kept at the Selawik School to update our data on the Selawik population census. We were by then referred to locally as "the Nigraqmiut," the people living on the Nigraq. Our house was the only house next to that channel. We felt honored to be incorporated into the map of the community's conceptual landscape. The warm greeting from a young boy, "Welcome back home to Selawik," and Douglas's invitation to be a judge on the Selawik Fourth of July baby contest were touching moments.

On our seventh return, toward the end of May 1981, we participated in two rural development projects. Douglas was first tasked to conduct an archaeological site survey prior to the development of a Selawik farm, supported by Rural Ventures, Inc. funds that the Northwest Arctic Native Association (NANA) had acquired. The second project was an archaeological field school, funded by the Comprehensive Employment Training Act (CETA), to teach Selawik high school students that history does exist in their village. The archaeology class was followed by oral history and museology training and the creation of a museum display of the objects excavated in the glass cabinets in the Selawik School's gym. The site selected for the excavation was the location of the first Selawik schoolhouse, built in 1908, on the Nigraq channel just opposite our house. We rowed to class. Seven students participated.

Douglas continued with his Selawik archaeological research in the summer of 1994 at Kuutchiaq, approximately forty miles upriver from the village, partly funded by the Northwest Arctic Borough. While the archaeology team, which included four Selawik field assistants, a boatman, and a cook excavated, for a month, Wanni stayed in the village to continue her ethnographic and folkloric studies, this time concentrating on the transformations that had occurred since our earlier visits. The children we had met in 1968 had become young adults. Some were married with children, some working in jobs, a few tragically passed away from accidental drowning or suicide. After gaining first-class city status in 1976, Selawik as village had reverted to being a second-class city again as discussed in chapter 10.

Our following archaeological excavation at Swift Water Place (Igliqtiqsiuġvigruaq) on the Kobuk disclosed that a few Selawik families had ancestral links to the Kobuk River site (Anderson and Anderson 2019). We returned to Selawik in the summer of 2017 to share our findings and interpretations with a talk in the Community Hall. Again, we met old friends and saw new families. Sadly, our yurt, our home away from home in Selawik, was falling down. May Walton, daughter of Douglas's hunting partner Arthur Skin, asked if her son could take the house down and use the wood to rebuild his house. We consented. Our outboard motorboat that we let the Skin family use became "Mama's boat." Allowing someone else to use what you no longer use or need is the Iñupiaq way.

This book bridges our lived experiences and archaeological and ethnographic research of eight field seasons in Selawik, from 1968 to 1994, with the historical and archaeological data on the early periods of Selawik village. It traces its history, the continuity of the past subsistence lifeway in the present, the interfacing of the traditional with the modern, and how specific events in the Selawik past have shaped the Selawik present. The contextual and ethnographic writing styles of part 2 of the book apply the experience-near, lived-experience, and sense-of-place approaches. They aim to portray the particularity of Iñupiaq life as was lived, sensed, and felt by Selawikers themselves and as experienced by us researchers. In addition, we aim to uncover multiple elements that make Selawik a living place (Feld and Basso 1996). Quoted observations, conversations, and comments acknowledge Iñupiaq insiders' narrative voices that speak about themselves, their viewpoints, their turmoil, and their constraints more eloquently than the researchers' words. The final chapter on self-determination analytically brings the Iñupiaq activist movement and Iñupiaq self-determination efforts into the indigeneity discourse.

We would like to thank all the people of Selawik who kindly shared their thoughts, experiences, and knowledge as well as their parents' oral histories that immeasurably assisted us in reconstructing Selawik's past and enlightened us to the Iñupiaq ways of living. Emma Norton kindly gave us the ledgers from Ferguson Store, which offered a glimpse into early trading post transactions in Selawik. Her mother, Nora, told us folktales, and we had many happy times with her family. William Sheldon taught Douglas how to make a sled. Nancy Starbuck taught us conversational Iñupiaq. Marjorie Ticket let us run an electric line from her house to our one-lightbulb house. Lenora Skin and Clara Ballot helped to keep their fish counts. Emma Ramoth made spring and summer parkas for Wanni. We thank the research funding from two organizations: the Wenner-Gren Foundation for the 1971–1972 ethnographic research and the Northwest Arctic Borough in support of the Selawik field assistants on the 1994 archaeological excavation at Kuutchiaq. To the reviewers of the manuscript and the editorial teams of Nate Bauer, Laura Furney, Rachel Fudge, and Tina Kachele of the University of Alaska Press and University Press of Colorado, we truly appreciate your helpful feedback and your editorial expertise.

WANNI W. ANDERSON AND DOUGLAS D. ANDERSON

IÑUPIAT OF THE SII

PART 1

Early Times

I

Introduction

The Siilaviŋmiut are a Northwest Alaskan Iñupiaq group who once lived in small settlements scattered along the waterways of the Selawik River and inter-lake region east of Selawik Lake. Their name is derived from the Iñupiaq words for place of the sheefish (*sii* = shee; *vik* or *vin* = place). The sheefish (*Stenodus leucichthys*) is the largest member of the whitefish subfamily of Coregoninae, also called *inconnu* (unknown fish) by early explorers.

Prior to the founding of the town of Selawik, the Siilaviŋmiut were comprised of two major population clusters that occupied the Selawik River Valley, sometimes referred to as Siilviim Kangianiġmiut (people of the upper river area) and the Kiitaaġmiut (people of the lower-river and inter-lake area). For at least the last century, the people have had close contacts with their relatives along the Kobuk River to the north and the Buckland River to the southwest. They also maintained close contact with relatives along the coast around Kotzebue Sound, where they traveled annually to hunt seals, fish for salmon, and conduct trade. Some individuals also maintained contact with Koyukon Indians by way of river valleys flowing into the Selawik River from the south.

Lying roughly between 156°30' and 160°20' west longitude and 66°00' and 67°00' north latitude, the Selawik River drainage system straddles the latitude of the Arctic Circle as the river flows westward into Kotzebue Sound. It is flanked on the north by the Waring Mountains and Hockley Hills that separate it from the lower Kobuk River Valley, on the southwest by the Selawik Hills that separate it from the

https://doi.org/10.5876/9781646426065.c001

Koyukuk River system, and on the east by the Lockwood Hills that separate it from the upper Kobuk and Koyukuk Rivers.

The upper reaches of the Selawik River valley include the Kugarak (Kuugruaq) and Tagraġvik, the two major tributaries. Here, the Selawik and much of the Kuugruaq and Tagraġvik Rivers flow through thick reworked deposits of recent and fossil-bearing glacial age riverine silts. For much of the area, the drainage pattern is comprised of short, slow-moving streams that drain myriad lakes. Where they enter the main river, the streams have cut small channels that appear to a traveler along the river as nicks in a monotonously featureless riverbank. In addition to the sheefish that inhabit the main river and tributaries, several species of smaller whitefish migrate between the lakes and the river along these small connecting streams. It is here that many Siilaviŋmiut families used to situate their summer and winter settlements. The remains of former campsites and dwellings are so common at these spots that an archaeologist can expect to find a site wherever one of these nicks in the riverbank occurs.

The lower Selawik region includes Kuugruaq (Kugarak in the map) and Tagraġvik and myriad small streams and lakes that lie between (figure 1.2). The lakes teem with whitefish and pike, and in summers they provide major nesting areas for waterfowl. In this region the preferred settlement localities were at the outlets of streams entering the many tiny lakes; few settlements were located directly along the shores of the two large lakes.

THE PROTO-HISTORY OF SELAWIK

At present we have no direct information about the earliest prehistoric residents of the Selawik River drainage system. Circumstantial evidence from adjoining areas suggests that people had already inhabited the region by the end of the last Ice Age. The best indications come from Onion Portage on the Kobuk River (D. Anderson 1988; Giddings 1967) and Trail Creek Caves on Seward Peninsula (Larsen 1968), where the earliest archaeological remains are known to be at least 10,000 years old. The only comparable archaeological remains in the Selawik drainage itself are a few undated flake stone scatters and implements from the Rabbit Mountain area of the Kuugruaq River (Anderson and Anderson 1977).

The term *proto-history* here refers to the period prior to European contact and the arrival of the Western material culture. As recorded in written history and discussed in the next chapter, the first white person to set foot in the Selawik River was John Simpson. The first European material culture discovered archaeologically so far was a part of a shotgun, excavated at Fox River in lower Selawik by Douglas Anderson's archaeological field school in 1976.

Initial proto-historical archaeological research of the area began with the search for and documentation of abandoned settlements and subsistence use areas. Accompanied by local residents who were able to pinpoint the sites on the survey, Douglas recorded seventy-three former habitation sites: fifty-two winter settlements, twenty-two summer fish camps, four fall fish camps, and nine spring muskrat camps (Anderson and Anderson 1977). Most of these sites were occupied before the founding of Selawik village. Doug identified use areas away from the settlements by focusing on names that Selawik residents have attached to various locations. Most points of interest, locations of subsistence resources, places connected to historic events, or places with unusual topographic features were named by their meanings related to the resource or subsistence activity carried out around the area (Anderson and Anderson 1970). Many of the elder residents could relate stories and discussions that they had had with their parents about these locations. These recollections, rich in detail about the camps, seasonal subsistence rounds, and Iñupiaq place names, serve as the oral history database for Douglas's reconstruction of the pre-village period.

Prior to the founding of Selawik village, area residents lived in small semipermanent communities scattered along the main course of the river, its two major tributaries (the Kuugruaq and Tagraġvik), and the inter-lake region between Selawik Lake and Inland Lake. Each group of residents was named after the area in which the groups located their winter settlements, such as Kuugaramiut (people of the Kuugruaq River), Katyaaġmiut (people of the forks of the confluence of the Tagraġvik and Selawik Rivers), and Kuutchiaġmiut (people of the Kuutchiaq River). According to the 1880 census, approximately 100 individuals lived in the region. A more accurate count in the 1900 US census placed the population at 367.

UPPER RIVER SETTLEMENTS

During the pre-village period, settlements were aggregates of family groupings that fostered interdependence among those related by kin ties living close to each other. Their main living settlements were the winter settlements, where they spent the long, severe winter months. Selection of locations for winter settlements involved two major considerations: proximity to prime fishing grounds and, at least prior to the caribou decline of the late nineteenth century (Skoog 1968), access to known caribou crossings and winter caribou feeding grounds.

Referred to as the "Kaniataaġmiut" by Arthur Skin, whose ancestors were upriver people, these people living at the mouths of small streams draining the lakes were able to procure fish coming out of the lakes. In many cases, the settlements also served as summer camps, making them essentially their year-round settlements. Once the winter quarters were set up and after freeze-up, upriver people would erect fish weirs across the slough-draining lakes to impound whitefish trying to swim downstream. The fish weirs provided them with their major winter fish supply. To harvest the fish, they would open the ice at the back of the weir and scoop up the fish by the dip net (*qalu*). The fish, heaped in mounds on the ice, would quickly freeze and become naturally preserved for the whole winter. Snowfalls after this time assisted the storage process, covering and insulating the fish piles against a too-solid freeze. Fish harvesting continued as long as the fishermen could break the ice around the weir. Where the stream was swift, fishing could continue until December. Whitefish, pike, and burbot played major roles in the diet of the upriver families.

Many upriver families set up their spring camps at or near outlets of small streams entering any of the myriad lakes in the region. The preferred campsites, located upstream from their winter houses, were to facilitate convenient rafting of the harvests back home. Where possible, they selected the camp grounds on the higher banks of a stream or a slough where the snow melted early and the grass formed a good dry mat for their tent floors. As oral history informed, to maintain easy communication between camps, another favored spring camp location was near the primary winter trail linking the Tagraġvik and lower Kuugruaq to the main channel of the Selawik River.

Some families were said to congregate at Kuutchauruk, a major summer fishing ground near the confluence of the Kuugruaq and Selawik Rivers, while others preferred locations along the upper Kuugruaq as their logistical locations for hunting muskrats while waiting for break-up.

In late March, when the river, lakes, and streams were still frozen, families would load their kayaks and camping gear onto the family sled and travel into the lake country away from the main channel to hunt muskrats. Their primary weapon at the time was the bow and arrow with blunt arrowheads.

The period of break-up between late May and early June signaled the beginning of summer activities. Starting earlier in the upper reaches of the Selawik River than in the lower reaches, by early June families in the upriver area were usually able to set up fish traps (*taluyat*) at the mouths of small streams draining lakes. Several families converged at locations where large fish traps could be built to set up joint fish camps. Other families, however, moved overland to the lakes south of the middle part of the Selawik River to establish smaller fish camps at the narrow exit streams of lakes. After setting up camps for their wives and mothers, the men frequently trekked to the upper Noatak to hunt the migrating caribou. Caribou hunting was exceptionally important since it afforded them the chance to obtain not only meat but summer hides and sinew thread for clothing and antler for a variety of manufactured items. People also engaged in trapping foxes, lynx, mink, and otter.

LOWER RIVER SETTLEMENTS

To our knowledge, the "Kiitaaġmiut," the lower river families, did not congregate in joint family camps as did the upriver families. Their winter settlements were generally established around locations where natural conditions created fast-flowing water that kept the ice cover thin, enabling them to continue fishing for a longer part of the winter. The best known of these locations were on the Fox River, along a short channel between Inland and Toklomarak Lakes, and on the Fish River, a swift-flowing clear-water stream at the northern edge of the lower Selawik River basin. Peninsulas, which often form along tidal currents around the inlets or outlets of larger lakes, were also favorite winter sites. In the early part of winter, women would set their nets under the ice away from shore, especially where currents eddied or where the water from several currents merged.

Lower river people set up spring camps on or around Selawik Lake, where they could hook for sheefish and pike. Many set up tents on the frozen lake itself near large ice ridges. Other families set up camps on the shores of the lake adjacent to stream outlets, such as at Mukuksok Point (Makkaksraq). The areas along willow- and alder-covered rivers like Fish River likewise provided good camping grounds because the alders could be cut for firewood and willows for construction materials, to be rafted back to the winter settlement. By mid-April, ducks and geese arriving from the south became their hunting targets.

Most summer sites were situated where the river edge bottom was flat and approximately four to eight feet deep near shore so that gill nets could be used. Some of the major summer settlements were located where open-water fish fences could be set up and used all summer. Later in the summer, between June and July, people could collect rhubarb, celery, and sourdock (*Rumex arcticus*), which grew profusely downriver. Also harvested were salmonberries, nagoon berries (*Rubis arcticus*, locally called strawberries), blueberries, and cranberries. The men remained in the vicinity of the camps to concentrate on hunting molting waterfowl near the mouth of Selawik River and hooking or spearing sheefish. For hooking, the major implement was the ivory or antler fish-lure hook (see figure 7.10), and for spearing a gill spear tipped with a *qemituk*, a pointed fish-shaped device thrust into the mouth of a shee and through its gills, was used.

Families with muskrat skins to trade would load their *umiat* onto sleds in order to continue to the coast following the ice-fishing season. At the coast, they camped at a traditional location northwest of Sisualik on Kotzebue Sound. From there, they engaged in salmon fishing, beluga hunting, and seal hunting with Buckland people. While there, the group also had the opportunity to participate in the annual trade fair with other Iñupiaq groups from the Noatak and Kobuk Rivers. The families boated back to their Selawik winter settlements by late August or early September.

To summarize, the annual subsistence round in the Selawik River system during the proto-historic period differed from settlement to settlement, depending on which resources were locally available. Generally speaking, upriver families were able to harvest a greater number and variety of terrestrial fur-bearing animals than their downriver relatives. The lower river families, on the other hand, had a better habitat for spring ice fishing at Selawik Lake and more ready access to trading with other Iñupiaq groups at the coast.

2

History before the Village Years

FIRST WESTERN CONTACTS

The earliest written records about the Selawik area come from Laavrentii Alekseevich Zagoskin, who in 1842–1843 explored the interior of Alaska on an expedition that was supposed to start from the Yukon River to Kotzebue Sound. He learned of the existence of the Selawik River from Natives whom he met at Khotylno/Kateel village on the Koyukuk River: "The old man Kitsykaka told us that there is a river in the extreme north, Tutleka-khotana or Tyneka-khotana, and that the people living along its upper waters have direct contact with the Naleygmyut [Malemiut]. The people living on the south coast of Norton Bay call this river 'Chilivik' " (Michael 1967:153).

Zagoskin did not enter the Selawik River drainage himself, despite the fact that had the expedition been successful, he might have taken the direct Tagraġvik–Selawik River route to Kotzebue Sound. He became ill on the trip and had to turn back from a point on the Kateel River not more than twenty-four miles southeast of the headwaters of the Tagraġvik.

The first European to enter the Selawik region was John Simpson, the surgeon from HMS *Plover*, who overwintered in Kotzebue Sound as part of the 1850–1851 search force for Sir John Franklin, explorer and commander of the ill-fated 1845 British expedition to complete the mapping of the Northwest Passage. Simpson made an exploratory sledge trip around Selawik Lake in May 1851. His account is as follows:

https://doi.org/10.5876/9781646426065.c002

This lake, which we called Sel'-a-wik, from the principal river falling into it, is about twenty-five miles in length from east to west, and fifteen in breadth from north to south, of an irregular oval form, and crossed in several places by lines of ice hummocks from six to eight, and, in a few instances, reaching as much as eleven feet, in height, indicating considerable pressure from winds and currents in the early part of the winter. The northern and southern shores appear to be formed of frozen earth resembling peat, varying from twenty to forty feet high, and along their foot were exposed occasional patches of sand and gravel already laid bare by the influence of the sun's rays. At two or three points the cliffs, becoming undermined by the action of the waves, were detached in large masses, exposing their peat-like formation from base to summit, intersected by numerous cracks, vertical, or nearly so, filled up by plates of ice from an eighth to half an inch in thickness, diminishing downwards, and at the top, where the ground was uncovered with snow, these cracks might be traced as narrow ruts, three to five inches deep, containing water.

Besides the numerous small streams falling into it from the higher ground on the north and south, the lake derives its waters from the Sel'-a-wik River, which flows into it by two mouths at the eastern extremity. This is a river of 190 feet in breadth, coming in from the eastward, and said, by the natives residing on its banks, to be about ten feet deep; but at the only point where we could get through the ice we found it seven feet three inches, with a soft muddy bottom. Ascending the river about a mile and a half to a rising ground, where there were several huts with a high stage for drying fish, and favored by very clear weather, I had an extensive view of the country around. To the south were the group of hills lying on the north bank of the Buckland River, and eastward from Eschotlz [*sic*] Bay, the nearest of which slopes directly down to the Sel'-a-wik Lake, and far in the distance to the E.S.E. a long range of peaks. On the north the view was bounded by a line of peaks about ten miles from the margin of the lake, running eastward, and at a long interval succeeded by a similar but very distant one to the E.N.E., but between these and the distant range to the E.S.E., as far as the eye could reach, there seemed to be only an interminable alluvial plain, containing numerous small lagoons, and supporting a few alders and willows. The few natives we met were to all appearance very poor, living in temporary sheds of deer skin. They do not even possess the usual clay cooking utensils, but boil their fish in wooden vessels by throwing in hot stones. They seem to subsist at this season entirely on fish, which they catch with a baited hook let down through holes in the ice. They exhibited great pleasure at seeing us, and behaved exceedingly well, making no attempts to pilfer, and freely bartered their fish for tobacco, but spoke of having been in great distress for want of food before the fishing season commenced. They informed us that there was a large village four days journey up the river, which it would be impossible to reach at this season, on account of the thaw, and that there was another village on the river Ko'-wuk, seven days journey northward beyond the hills, which, for the same reason, was at present unapproachable, without great risk, but beyond these they seemed to have no knowledge whatever of the country. Although we could find no trees growing in the vicinity, there was a good deal of driftwood about the banks of the river, twelve inches and under in diameter, which could hardly have been brought there otherwise than down the stream. On the north side of the lake there is a low point containing numerous small lagoons, now partially thawed, in which the waterfowl are collected in great numbers. Here we remarked a small solitary pine tree; the only one we saw growing near the lake. (Simpson 1852:91–93)

In the mid-nineteenth century, the entire region was impacted by the arrival of American whaling vessels that plied the waters of the Chukchi Sea and Arctic Ocean. Although the whaleships largely bypassed Northwest Alaska on their way to the whaling grounds off North Alaska, the Iñupiat, including the Siilaviŋmiut, were indirectly involved in commerce with them via Point Hope and Cape Prince of Wales Natives who traveled to the trading rendezvous around Kotzebue Sound.

After the US purchase of Alaska from Russia in 1867, Euro-American influence in Northwest Alaska was primarily in the hands of the US federal government and several missionary societies. The US government had two primary goals in governing the Iñupiat: maintaining law and order, and, somewhat later, providing education. The first goal was achieved through the US Marine Revenue Service, whose ships monitored the major coastal villages. Their aim was

to assist when disaster or shipwreck overtakes the [American] whalers, to search after missing vessels, to note the bearing of the different points of land, islands, etc., to determine the position of bars and reefs encountered, to keep a record of tides and currents, to take meteorological and astronomical observations for the benefit of commerce, to investigate scientific phenomena, and inquire into the mode of life, political and social relations of the native population, and make collections for the Smithsonian Institution, and to perform many other services beneficial to commerce, science, and humanity. (US Bureau of Education, 1893)

The second goal of the federal government—to govern and to "civilize" the Native—was carried out through two strategies that had already been developed elsewhere among other Native American Indigenous groups: settling the scattered groups into manageable enclaves and schooling.

By the 1880s, Northwest Alaska must have been seen as relatively safe for non-Natives to visit. The second explorer known to have traveled through the Selawik area was Captain Johan Adrian Jacobsen, a Norwegian sent by the Königliches Museum für Völkerkunde in Berlin, to make a collection along the northwestern coast of North America. In 1882–1883, Jacobsen journeyed by sledge and Native guide from Koyuk across Seward Peninsula to Escholtz Bay, and from there to the Selawik Lake area, where he met some Siilaviŋmiut who sold him a variety of ethnographic items (Jacobsen [1884] 1977). This ethnographic collection is now stored at the Museum für Völkerkunde.

The following year, Ensign J. L. Purcell of the 1884–1885 Naval Explorations in Alaska conducted a brief trip to Selawik Lake at the behest of expedition leader Lieutenant George M. Stoney. Purcell, accompanied by two Iñupiat named Riley and Ounalana, entered the lake on August 22 and over the course of the next two days circumnavigated much of its shores (Stoney 1900). He noted discovering the mouth of the Selawik River as well as another river and two lakes, one of which was Inland Lake. It is unclear whether he actually entered the Selawik River itself, however, since his account better fits the entrance to Toklamaruk and Inland Lakes, neither of which connected with Selawik River at the time.

From his description, it appears that, in fact, Purcell had entered a small stream through a series of "many lagoons communicating with the rivers" that connected Selawik Lake to Inland Lake. He referred to the Natives he came across as "Selawik Indians."

> The next morning I started up this river and reached the inland lake, passing, in the meantime, through a smaller lake, the expansion of the river. The river has its source in Inland Lake and flows W. by S. in a very winding course for two miles, where it expands into the abovementioned small lake four miles long and two miles wide, contracting afterwards to its regular width of seventy-five yards. It runs its winding course three miles more and discharges into Selawik Lake by two mouths about a mile apart. The depth, of eight feet to five fathoms; the banks are covered with grass to the water's edge; also, there is a good deal of brushwood on them. Here are scattered about and a number of graves were noticed, most of them about two years old. Only one family was found living on the river, consisting of a young native twenty-five years old, his wife twenty years old, and a small boy of three. They seemed hardy, active and intelligent, and in habits and appearances like those of the Putnam [Kobuk]. Their hut was mound-shaped, made of brushwood covered with grass and mud, with an entrance through a small hole next to the ground. The height of the house was five feet in the center and the diameter about six feet. Scattered about were a few spears for catching fish and birds. We were compelled to boil them, as the natives objected to frying or broiling because to do so would make the fish leave the river and never return. Many Selawik Indians live on this river and all come here to fish in September, when the river is full of fish and at this time they lay in their winter supply. (Stoney 1900:546)

Figure 2.1. George M. Stoney, leader of the 1884–1885 Naval Explorations in Alaska team.

George Stoney himself (figure 2.1) explored the river in December 1884, but we have not found his original account of that trip.
He again explored the Selawik area in 1885 and 1896:

On December 29th, 1885, I left Fort Cosmos with three natives, two sleds, sixteen dogs, and provisions and outfit for ten days. My object was to explore the country between the Putnam River and Selawik Lake, and to see if there was a Selawik River. The route followed led across the southern side of the Putnam valley, through a pass over a ridge of hills, 400 feet high, into the Selawik valley. The country was rolling tundra land, generally bare, with a scant growth on the banks of the small streams and around the lakes. Finding a Selawik River, I traced its course for many miles. I cut through the ice and found no appreciable current, but water deep enough to float the Explorer [Stoney's boat used in open water for exploring the rivers] when the river broke. A range of mountains 2000 to 3000 feet high, running in spurs with high hills between, makes the watershed between the Putnam and Selawik Rivers. The natives of the Selawik are miserably poor and badly clad. They get little meat, as few deer are found in the neighboring mountains, so their main food is fish and the berries they gather in autumn. Their habits and customs are like those of the Putnam natives. The thermometer ranging between −60° and −70° F.; and also because only a little wood was procurable for making firs. The dogs suffered terribly, their feet cracking open and bleeding with every step. I was compelled to employ natives to drag the sleds where the roads were heavy. (Stoney 1900:571–572)

For the next decade Siilaviŋmiut were in frequent contact with Euro-Americans, largely during the annual summer rendezvous at Kotzebue. But it is uncertain which or how many foreigners actually visited the Siilaviŋmiut in their home territory during the last decade of the nineteenth century.

This was also the period in which missionary societies became active in the region. The first mission in Northwest Alaska was at Cape Prince of Wales, established in 1890. It was soon followed by the arrival of numerous missions to other coastal villages.

ESTABLISHING GOVERNMENT AUTHORITY IN NORTHWEST ALASKA

The latter part of the nineteenth century ushered in major changes for the Siilaviŋmiut, as they did for other Iñupiaq families throughout Northwest Alaska. In the 1890s, the US government began to assert control over the region by establishing schools and encouraging missionaries and private traders to operate in the area. The mandate for educating Natives was written in the Organic Act of 1884, Section 13, which stipulated that:

The Secretary of the Interior shall make needful and proper provision for the education of the children of school age in the Territory of Alaska, without reference to race, until such time as permanent provision shall be made for the same, and the sum of twenty-five thousand dollars, or so much thereof as may be necessary is hereby appropriated for this purpose.

As is so often the case, however, the mandate was undermined by the government's failure to provide adequate funds for the purpose. The solution was to seek assistance from nongovernmental organizations. Encouraged by Sheldon Jackson, Presbyterian minister and director of education for Alaska, the government contracted with missionary societies, which were eager to establish footholds in the region for proselytizing and could supply teachers, to set up schools (Barnhardt,

2001). To keep church and state separate, as required by US law, missionary societies recruited married couples, one spouse to serve as government teacher and the other as missionary. The aims of the government and the missionary societies therefore overlapped to a considerable extent. Both wanted to "civilize the Natives," which meant teaching them a way of life oriented around Christian values. The government also wanted to make Natives responsible, patriotic citizens who could function in the modern world; the missionaries wanted to make Natives "moral" persons who aspired to a sin-free life in alignment with Christian beliefs. Although the schools were generally effective in educating Iñupiat, the separation of the educational and religious roles was not really achievable in that husband and wife both simultaneously served as missionary and teacher. Thus, even though schools and missions were officially kept distinct, they were intimately interlinked from the beginning.

The close link between government schools and missionaries continued for at least the next two decades. For the Iñupiat, there was never any real distinction between church and state. They perceived the teacher/missionary couple as part of the same enterprise, which in fact they were in all respects.

Around Kotzebue Sound, the first school and mission station was established at the northern tip of Baldwin Peninsula under the auspices of the California Society of Friends (California Quakers). The selection of this mission society was the result of an arrangement formulated by the missionary societies at an ecumenical convention in 1880 that allotted different denominations exclusive rights to proselytize in different parts of Alaska. The California Quakers were assigned the Kotzebue Sound region in 1896.

The arrival of the California Friends missionaries Robert and Carrie Samms in 1897 ushered in profound changes throughout Northwest Alaska. Interestingly, the Samms were not the first missionaries in the region. By 1896, at least one missionary, Uyagaq, an Iñupiaq often referred to as Mr. Rock from the Swedish Evangelical Mission in Unalakleet, was already proselytizing along the lower part of the Selawik valley. In fact, when the Friends missionaries arrived at Kotzebue Sound in August 1897, Uyagaq was there to meet them. It is not clear whether he had explicitly traveled from Selawik to Kotzebue to greet the Samms or if it was a chance meeting. Nevertheless, Uyagaq devoted considerable time and effort to help them get established. Over the course of the following two years or more, he, along with several Siilaviŋmiut, frequently visited the Kotzebue mission (Samms 1898).

Some of Uyagaq's history is known and detailed by Arthur O. Roberts (1978), but many gaps exist, especially for the period after Uyagaq's arrival in Selawik. Uyagaq was born in 1876. His wife was Keketuk from Unalakleet. He had many relatives in Kotzebue and Sisualik, just north of the present-day city of Kotzebue. Uyagaq had made several missionary journeys to Selawik and elsewhere in the region, first with David Johnson, another missionary from Unalakleet, then with Stephen Ivanoff. Later, with his wife and children. Uyagaq lived and taught among the Siilaviŋmiut between 1893 and 1896 and also after 1898. Richard Jones, a Selawik elder who knew him, called Uyagaq "a prophet" (Roberts 1978:157). It is not known when or why Uyagaq ended up in Selawik, although some accounts say he was born there and others say that Selawik was his home. Neither is confirmed. We were not able to track down when or where he died or was buried.

In 1898, a gold rush to the Kobuk River brought about another impact on the lives of the northwestern Alaskan Iñupiat (Grinnell 1901). More than a thousand prospectors sailed to Kotzebue Sound and stampeded into the rumored goldfields along the rivers. They largely bypassed the Selawik Valley, as might be expected given the near absence of bedrock exposures there. But at least a few prospectors did indeed find their way into the upper part of the Selawik valley. According to some Selawik elders, they arrived first at Tivli on the Kuutchiaq River and then moved to Katyaak at the mouth of the Tagraġvik River, where they wintered. By 1900 or 1901 most of these men died, according to the oral account that Douglas obtained from Elmer Ballot of Selawik. Survivors boated down the Selawik to Kotzebue (Lee, Sampson, and Tennant 1989). Douglas's archaeological search for traces of these prospectors has thus far failed to yield results.

Despite the sudden surge of Western commodities brought into the region by the prospectors, there seems to have been little impact on the lifeways of the Siilaviŋmiut at the time. For example, during the first part of May 1899, as many as seven groups of Siilaviŋmiut went to Kotzebue and from there to Sisualik to hunt and trade as had been their practice for generations.

Following the establishment of a school and mission in Kotzebue in 1897, the government, partly if not largely at Robert Samms's urging, began to expand into the interior of Northwest Alaska. The effort was complicated, however, by the complete absence of established villages in which to situate the schools. This meant that the government first had to come up with other inducements to bring the scattered residents together. Founding a local school for the Native children became an expedient strategy.

3

Founding of Selawik Village

The federal government's project for Selawik started in 1907. At the behest of A. N. Evans, assistant superintendent of schools for the Northern District, the first formal census of the Selawik River area was recorded by Kotzebue native John Armstrong (Punneck). According to Armstrong, the entire Selawik area consisted of sixty-four men, sixty-six women, and ninety-three children. In a December 17, 1907, letter to the commissioner of education in Washington, DC, encouraging the establishment of a school on the Selawik River, Evans wrote: "These [Iñupiat living in the Selawik area] are scattered in three different settlements but declare that they will move to the place at which a school will be built, should the department decide to place a school on the river" (US Bureau of Education 1908–1919).

It is unclear to which three settlements Evans was referring, but at least two of them were likely in the lower river area. In his enthusiasm for the project, Evans declared that the Selawik, as well as the Noatak where he was also proposing to establish a school, was "well-timbered [which it is not] and the entire region is well stocked with the game and the river with fish."

Although it is difficult to specify exactly why the government wanted to set up schools in the remote interiors of Northwest Alaska, one apparent reason was to confine the interior populations to their home areas so they would not migrate into coastal villages. As stated by Evans, "It is advisable to keep the natives out away from the towns [for example, Kotzebue] and wherever the natives have schools, they have little desire to go to the towns except for trading purposes and then return to

https://doi.org/10.5876/9781646426065.c003

their homes." The government project was encouraged by Director of Education Sheldon Jackson, as well as the mission societies, which were eager to begin proselytizing the riverine Iñupiat of Northwest Alaska.

The location for the Selawik school was largely determined by the recommendations of several local Iñupiat. Evans stated, "The best location for buildings on these rivers is hard to determine at present and before writing on this subject prefer to wait until I see the rivers." The men who advised Evans in his selection included Kinyoruk/Skotok (grandfather of Effie Ramoth), who was already known to Robert Samms in Kotzebue, and four or five heads of the families from the lower part of the Selawik River: Yiyee Foster, Ikik Sheldon, Kowikte Foxglove, Caumauk Young, and Pesak (Charlie Smith's father).

They chose a part of the lower river where good winter and summer fish netting sites were abundant and where alder and willow for firewood grew. It was also the section of the river closest to the coastal supply center at Kotzebue. The spot picked out for the school was the outlet of a small channel, the Nigraq, that emptied into the Selawik River just below Akuliġaq (*akuliaq* means the ridge between the brows, middle), a large island in the main channel of the river. This location—the island and adjacent banks of the main river—is the site of the present-day city of Selawik.

The schoolhouse was erected on the northern bank of the Nigraq, close to the water's edge. The building, slated to be a combined schoolhouse and teacher's residence (according to a May 27, 1908, letter from Commissioner Elmer Ellsworth Brown), was originally to be constructed of lumber purchased from the Alaska Mercantile Company in Nome and shipped there through Kotzebue (US Bureau of Education, Alaska Division n.d.). But the shipment of supplies from Kotzebue to Selawik was delayed, so the five men who had advised Evans took it upon themselves to construct the schoolhouse out of logs rafted from the Fish River, a small stream north of Selawik. It appeared, however, that from the outset the building they had put up was intended to be temporary. According to Evans in a December 25, 1908, letter:

> Under this circumstance [the delay in receiving building supplies] Mr. and
> Mrs. Sickles, the teachers, were left without shelter for the winter, and it seemed
> advisable to erect a temporary cabin for them to live in, and with the assistance of
> natives to put up a temporary building for the school. The logs for the cabin were
> loaned to the teachers by a native without charge, and the only cost was for the erec-
> tion of the cabin, $34.00. It was necessary to get logs for the school house, making
> the cost of this temporary building $20.00. It is roughly constructed and sodded over.
> All this work was done after the freeze-up. (US Bureau of Education 1908–1919)

The men from the five families involved also built their own winter homes adjacent to the teacher's cabin, all working together on each house. Ikik Sheldon,

Figure 3.1. High school students participating in the Selawik archaeological field school, 1981.

however, opted to build his house on the opposite bank of the Nigraq, directly across from the schoolhouse. It was coincidentally at his house site that we were later allowed to build our house in 1969. Other families from the region whose children were to attend the first school class set up their tents across from the school on the southern side of the Nigraq.

Although we have no details on design of the schoolhouse, it was reportedly based on a *kargi* plan, known locally as a "seven-family house." Elmer Ballot informed us that it was constructed as a log house much larger in size than a normal Iñupiaq home. It served concurrently as the church and residence of the first missionary/teacher couple, Leslie G. and Frances M. Sickles.

In 1981, to locate the remains of this original 1908 schoolhouse settlement, we conducted an archaeological field school involving the survey and excavation of the site with Selawik High School students (figure 3.1).

We found traces of the settlement, which included five deep house pits and a large leveled area that may have been a surface dwelling. The house pits, two of which were about twenty square feet, were partially slumped in. Archaeological excavations of the leveled area revealed a rectangular floor area that may have been a surface dwelling (Anderson 2023) (figure 3.2). Archaeological finds indicating

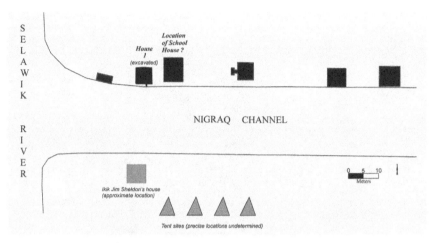

Figure 3.2. Location of the first school settlement at Nigraq.

the subsistence lifeway of the Native families that lived there included a net sinker, ivory fishhook, dog chain links, stone oil lamp, wooden spoon, and pieces of pottery. Emma Skin, one of the surviving pupils from that first school, informed us that the first school class consisted of herself, Topsy Ramoth, Charlie Smith, Richard Jones, Flora Cleveland, Tommy Skin, Luke Goode, Joe and Jim Foxglove, Lydia, and other students whose names she could not recall (Anderson and Anderson, field notes 1981). Emma said that at school there was an open tin can nailed to a house post to store pencils.

Shortly into the first school year, it was discovered that the location was not suitable: according to the School Report of June 30, 1910, "the old school house was low and water came in [the] schoolhouse and dwelling" (US Bureau of Education 1908–1919). As a result, in 1909, the school building—logs and all—was relocated to a high bank on the western side of the main river, which remains the present location of the Selawik School. The building was placed in the center of a 277.8-foot-by-627-foot area, officially set aside as a "reservation of the United States Public School, Selawik." The building supplies that had been scheduled for 1908 finally arrived in 1909 and were used to construct the school and teacher's residence at the new location. By October, the school was open, and "there was great joy over the new building as well as the books, charts and school equipment" (School Report, 1910, US Bureau of Education 1908–1919).

The five families at the original schoolhouse site on the Nigraq also relocated to the new school area in locations still occupied today by their descendants. Oral accounts of the surviving first class of students informed that, by 1910, an additional eight families had constructed their homes in or adjacent to the reservation, all with glass windows and most with planked floors. Other families began to settle directly across the river on Akuliġaq Island. Within a year or two, most of the families in the lower Selawik region had resettled in the vicinity of the village. Soon, families from the upper reaches of the river also began to move in, mostly onto the island.

From the oral historical sources, we can conclude that the early settlement pattern of Selawik was demarcated by the school side being populated at the very beginning by the lower-river founding families and on the island by the upriver people. Together, these families were the first residents of the newly formed Selawik community, joined later by other emigrants from the Kobuk River and in-marrying spouses within the region. Selawik grew into a sizable settlement, today the largest in the region outside the coastal city of Kotzebue.

The first teacher/missionary couple selected by the California Quaker Friends Mission for Selawik, Leslie G. and Frances M. Sickles, were from Everett, Washington. They arrived during the summer of 1908 after landing a few weeks earlier in Kotzebue by the US Marine Revenue Cutter *Bear*. During the three years that the Sickles were stationed in Selawik, they played a key role in the affairs of this nascent village.

From the Sickles' standpoint, their assigned purpose centered upon teaching Christian religious values to adults and practical skills to children. The children were taught to read, write, calculate, and, most importantly, to speak English. Speaking Iñupiaq in school was strictly prohibited, with infractions punishable by physical or verbal reprimand liberally meted out. In fact, the trauma of reprimand was so deeply felt that several of the city elders we talked with over the years who were students at the time argued against the introduction of the bilingual programs into the Selawik School in 1972 on the grounds that "we had suffered so much having to learn English, why should we have our children suffer learning Iñupiaq?" In other words, why learn the Iñupiaq language now when speaking this mother tongue was discouraged and punished in their generation? The dominant view among the Siilaviŋmiut, however, is that speaking Iñupiaq is very important and a key to maintaining cultural identity.

The Sickles substituted Iñupiaq music with Western music, teaching schoolchildren to play Western musical instruments "to keep the young out of mischief." The pupils must have been avid learners, since by the later part of the winter of 1912, they had an orchestra of a violin, mandolin, and guitars which "played for entertainments, school and church work" (figure 3.3).

Despite severe discipline, Selawik pupils by and large studied well in school. For those who did not live in the village, the adults' challenge was to balance their vital

Figure 3.3. Schoolchildren with their musical instruments in front of the second schoolhouse, 1912 (Archives, University of Alaska). Emma Skin plays the guitar, Kalmirak plays the mandolin, and Charlie Smith plays the violin. In the back row are William Sheldon's brother and Leslie Young (identified by Emma Skin).

full-time Iñupiaq subsistence life with the government-imposed school schedule for their children. The dilemma was especially hard for those from the upriver area, since they were displaced farthest from their traditional hunting and fishing grounds. Families from the lower river area did not have the same problem, since they could still remain in their traditional winter homes, continue their usual subsistence rounds, and send the children to school from there. Over time, however, even these families chose to resettle in the village.

With more Siilaviŋmiut families moving into the village, the teacher/missionary couple became the primary link between the people of the region and the government. The teachers were the go-to persons in case of sickness or accident or for issues that involved relations beyond the village. These roles continued to dominate the village organizational structure for the next twenty years. What was implemented in Selawik was modeled after a small town in the Euro-American United States where the church played a critical role. Selawik village leaders, who were dominant figures in the Friends Church, formed the village council that met regularly to manage village affairs. Mr. Sickles served as village clerk and recorder of minutes. The meetings were surprisingly formal and businesslike. Below are two examples of the minutes of the meetings on June 20, 1910, and October 3, 1910.

> The Selawik Eskimo Business meeting [June 20] was held at Selawik Lake as all natives were scattered there and opened by songs and prayer.
>
> Previous minutes were read and the mind of all to accept as read. The overseers with the aid of three more were appointed to oversee and help the Christian work while at Kotzebue.
>
> Birth and death report was given by Lester and approved as read. The committee to move the log school house on the reservation reported all finished, all responded to work and quickly was transferred.
>
> It was the mind of the meeting that the overseers see that the organ be sent to Selawik safely by best means possible. Tusolia volunteered to make a handle for some tool that belonged to an old woman that got broke in moving logs. Some time was used answering questions and meeting closed by song and prayer.

And:

> The Selawik Eskimo Business meeting [October 3] opened at 6:30 by songs 90–42 and prayers by many. A few number were present but so many were hunting. Boklook brought a copy of game laws so took some time to explain. It was the mind to write for an extension of time on muskrat hunting season.
>
> A few minutes to explain the need of work shop also their duty to build. Previous minutes were read and approved. Birth and Death report was given by Sister and approved as read.
>
> A partial report was given of the meeting at Kotzebue, but a full report be expected next meeting. A report of cost and expense of organ was given as: Cost $61,75.
>
> A live of talk was given along cleaning, moral etc. After which the meeting closed. (Minutes of the Selawik Eskimo Business meeting, mimeographed copy, California Yearly Meeting of Friends Church Archives, Selawik)

The Friends Church organizations in the region also developed particular proselytizing practices that went a long way toward cementing their place in the region and fostering relations between Kotzebue and the villages on the Kobuk, Noatak, and Selawik Rivers. The first was the "gospel trip," in which members of one village travel to another village to perform songs and provide individual testimonials. This tradition was already in effect by 1914 and continues today. Another church activity, appealing to the Iñupiaq sense of togetherness, was the gathering of villagers at the quarterly and yearly meetings of Friends in various villages in the region. Later, training and appointments of Iñupiaq pastors

TABLE 3.1. Population of Selawik and scattered residents by year.

Year	Living in Selawik	Scattered population	Year	Living in Selawik	Scattered population
1913	144	81	1922	240	30
1915	175	50	1926	177	62
1916	181	40	1928	171	98
1917	190	55	1929	250	24
1918	192	57	1931	220	55
1920	200	55			

Compiled from the annual reports of the California Yearly Meeting of Friends Church Archives, Selawik.

who could conduct the church service in Iñupiaq further bonded the Friends Church to its congregation. The Kobuk, Selawik, and Noatak became Quaker religious territory.

As in other parts of Northwest Alaska, local Iñupiat perceived the founding of the village, the school, and the church as a single interrelated event. Even after the federal government no longer contracted with the missionary societies for teacher/missionaries, the Quaker influence in Selawik remained strong in the village government as well as in the school. With few exceptions, the civilian teachers contracted by the government continued to be drawn from the Society of Friends in America well into the 1930s.

For thirty years after the founding of the village, the population of Selawik varied by season. Most Siilaviŋmiut lived in the village during winter but vacated it in late spring and summer to go to their camps for fishing and muskrat hunting or to Kotzebue for sealing or trade. Fluctuations in the village population between 1913 and 1920 (table 3.1) also indicate that families relocated to other areas when needed.

Intermittently between 1915 and 1950, several families resettled away from the village in order to trap, prompted by the high fur prices some years and the need for cash or skins to barter at the newly established trading posts and stores. Population also fluctuated as people tried to avoid the scourge of sickness that hit the village and the region periodically. Some of these families lived in winter houses upriver as recently as 1955.

In general, however, there has been a strong tendency for increasing numbers of Siilaviŋmiut to reside in the village year-round. Many nowadays do not even maintain individual fish camps elsewhere, because families want to keep children in school and to be near the stores and the post office.

TO MOVE OR NOT TO MOVE THE VILLAGE

Despite the advantage of situating the village in the fish-rich lower part of the Selawik River, some villagers soon became unhappy with its location. In contrast to teacher Robert Samms's school report of 1914 that the people were pleased with how things were progressing, by 1916 the situation seemed to have changed. According to the school report [teacher's name is illegible], of June 30, 1916,

> [Selawik] is a village most unfortunately situated, a great part of it is at this time being under water. There has been a great deal of agitation on the part of the natives in favor of removing the school to a more desirable locality. During the winter months much of the time that the Eskimo should spend in trapping and hunting he must devote to the task of fetching in wood, and each year this is becoming more of a problem, the nearest timber of any consequence being at least 30 miles from the village. In the winter it is a windswept stormy place, and in the spring, summer and fall, the village is a mud hole fit only for mosquitos and ducks.

As a result of the arguments to move the village, people delayed building or renovating their homes, apparently making living conditions even less comfortable. The effort to relocate the village continued for several years. In the June 30, 1919, annual report, government teacher Sylvester Chance reported:

> For years teachers and natives have desired to move, but thus far no location has been found which satisfies. In the fall of 1917, Mr. Jones, the teacher, myself, and a committee representing the Eskimos went up Selawik River and chose what we thought was a much better location near timber. The next spring the river was higher than usual and piled ice all over the place we had chosen for the village site. The objection has since been made that the fish supply in the fall and winter is uncertain, though I think this objection is unfortunate. (US Bureau of Education 1908–1919)

The chosen location was a nicely wooded and dry hillside area known as Upiṅġivik, one of the loveliest spots along the entire river. However, after failing to secure an upriver site in 1917, the effort to move the village appeared to have waned, and subsequent government reports no longer mention efforts for a move.

4

Trade Fair with Indians[1]

In 1912, Selawik experienced a unique event, possibly the last of similar happenings rooted in the remote past. This was a trade fair with the Indians, specifically the Koyukon Athapaskans, organized by Matoolik Skin (Andrew Skin's father), an upriver resident. According to his nephew Arthur Skin, Matoolik, who lived up the Kuugruaq, and his partner Harry Mitchell, who lived up the Tagraġvik, were quite familiar with the Indians from the Kateel River, a branch of the Koyukuk, a major tributary in the Yukon River.

The Selawik fair was said to be a reciprocal event for an earlier potlatch that was held two years before at Koyukuk in December 1910, which several Selawik Iñupiat had attended. That earlier Indian potlatch under the leadership of the Koyukuk Chief Paul was a three-week event in which the Koyukuk village hosted Athapaskan tribes from as far away as Nulato, Tanana, and Kokrines on the Yukon River as well as "Eskimos from Selawik River, who came to trade" (Letter dated December 31, 1910, to the Supply and Dispersing Office, US Bureau of Education, Alaska Division n.d.).

Several Selawik elders, including Johnnie Foster, Flora Cleveland, Topsy Ramoth, Billy Neal, and Kotzebue residents Freida and Charlie Goodwin, remembered the trade fair in Selawik and provided eye-witness accounts. The Goodwins described the fair as a potlatch or a trade dance, which can be referred to in anthropological

---

1. For a discussion of the terms Inupiat, Eskimo, and Indian, see Anderson 2023.

https://doi.org/10.5876/9781646426065.c004

Figure 4.1.
Willie Goodwin,
1966.

terms as a "messenger feast." The Selawik messenger in this last trade fair with the
Indians was Charlie Goodwin (Iyugak, father of Willie Goodwin; figure 4.1), who
was an upriver resident at the time. The messenger from the host community had a
significant role of informing people in other villages what items were to be brought
to the trade fair.

Charlie Goodwin narrated that his messenger trip to the Indian country took
several weeks. He had to travel as far south as the Yukon, just above Nulato. In his
interview with Douglas in 1972, Charlie provided a fascinating account of the ritu-
alized procedures of the invitation to the trade fair:

> When I entered an Indian village I had to go in to a specific house with my hood
> pulled over my eyes, then lay down in the bedroll with my face covered and said
> nothing. The people in the house went out and shouted "someone is visiting us *hi*
> *hi*!" The shout would travel around the village. Then I could get up and ate with the
> family. The husband then asked his wife "Do you have new mukluks for Charlie?"
> For the invitation I took with me a (willow?) staff of about 1 ½ feet with a series of

rings cut out around it. I stood straight, grasped the staff with my thumb and index finger just below one of the rings, stamped my feet, and shouted: "That man (name of a particular person from Selawik) wants so and so (name of a person in the Indian village) to come. Do not fail! Bring (e.g.) some fur (name of fur) or (some other item) to trade, and so on." This went on until I said what I was supposed to say for every ring on the staff. At least one of the villages I visited held a three-day dance for the occasion.

When I returned to Selawik I was supposed to sneak back into the village without anyone seeing me. Freida, my wife said she had kept looking for me. Later, when she saw the Indians arriving with several dog teams, she was afraid of them. (D. Anderson interview with Charlie and Freida Goodwin, Kotzebue, May 24, 1971)

Attracted by an opportunity to trade directly with the Indians, or as Kitty Foster put it, "a chance to see Indians," Iñupiat from Kotzebue and from other parts of Northwest Alaska traveled to Selawik for the event.

As was the tradition among the Iñupiat for hosting intercommunity events, Selawik villagers prepared for the fair for several months in advance, laying in an extra supply of fish to feed incoming visitors. The supply was largely exhausted by the end of the week of the feast, and for several months thereafter, Selawik families suffered their own food shortages. The potlatch was held in the village at the *kargi*, a building with two tiers of benches around the walls, located on Akuliġaq Island, just north of the present-day Friends Church. The Indians arrived in several dog teams.

In a government school report submitted just before the event, the missionary/teacher Leslie Sickles gave his pronouncement: "We have many Kotzebue natives here and from other points. I fear they are here anticipating a glorious time this winter by having a trade dance and all the side shows which accompany such an affair." In a follow-up report, in July 1912, he wrote, "While here they [the Indians] had liquor and gambled for money and skins."

Flora Cleveland, who was a teenager at the time, informed Douglas that the fair also included dancing. The teachers, the Sickles, had forbidden Iñupiaq Christians to participate, and fearing God's wrath, Flora did not dare join the festivity. But her grandmother and mother ignored the Sickles and danced all night. Selawik's converted religious leaders saw these as unsavory behaviors, and as a result they prohibited future Indian trade fairs from being organized in Selawik. The rare ethnic, economic, and social exchange opportunities that had existed between these two ethnic groups through the event were shortchanged.

As is implied by Charlie Goodwin's oral history account, it appears that Selawik and Koyukon Indians must have been quite knowledgeable about each other, even to the extent of knowing each other's names, as indicated in the trading item specifi-cations mentioned above. But relations with the Indians (Koyukon) were not com-pletely without tension. According to the Selawik teacher Robert Samms in the June 30, 1914, school report, two years after the trade fair, "An Indian scare caused many [Selawik families] to abandon their fishing places at a time when the fish were most abundant" (US Bureau of Education 1908–1919). It is interesting that we have yet to find a single documented incidence of actual fighting between the Indians and the Siilaviŋmiut.

Individual Indian families from the Koyukuk continued to visit the Selawik River area well into the 1920s, but they confined their trade fair celebrations to Niliq, the settlement several miles upriver from Selawik. The account and perspec-tive of Madeline Solomon, a Koyukuk woman living in the vicinity of the Kateel River, collaborated Selawik Flora Cleveland's narrative.

> On the way from their camp on the Kateel, we had to lay over twenty-files miles
> from Selawik at Niliq. Niliq is where they would go for potlatches and dancing. They
> weren't allowed to have Eskimo dancing in their villages on account of the missionar-
> ies. They're still like that. They can't dance at Selawik. It's awful hard. They can't play
> no kind of cards, but, of course, they drink. (Madison and Yarber 1981)

5

Fur Trade and Early Trading Posts in Selawik

Shortly after the founding of the village, the Siilaviŋmiut entered a commercial world that connected them to newly arrived non-Native traders, especially from Kotzebue. The initial structure for the developing local economy centered on the fur trade, which provided residents with income in the form of fur credits for the purchase of Western goods.

Within three years of the founding of the village, a store was opened in Selawik by Matoolik Skin, an upriver hunter and fisherman who had been trading along the river and its tributaries. He was the community leader and organizer of the 1912 trade fair with the Indians. Matoolik's store, located near the northern end of Akuliġaq Island, was stocked with food, dry goods, and, to the dismay of the teacher/missionary Sickles, playing cards, pipes, and tobacco. The merchandise, which Matoolik boated up from Kotzebue, was obtained from trader John Berryman, one of the first store owners in Kotzebue, and included gunpowder and muzzle loaders. The opening of Matoolik's store introduced a new chapter in the history of Selawik village economics. It transitioned from the traditional Iñupiaq subsistence practices and intercommunity trading exchange system to semi-mercantile village economy, characterized by Joseph G Jorgensen (1990:134) as the selling of Native goods and labor for gain to foreign merchants. In the Selawik case, this economy included the selling of fur skins and pelts to buy Western commodities that the traders brought in. It laid the foundation for the later development of the cash economy within the village that characterize the region.

https://doi.org/10.5876/9781646426065.c005

Evidently Kotzebue was at the time a major transition point for the flow of Western goods into villages in Northwest Alaska. Another early trader in Kotzebue was William Shakespeare Levy, who, according to an unconfirmed account, was said to have briefly had a store on the Selawik River.

Around 1915, Berryman moved to expand his trading territory, opening an additional store in Selawik. Even though he did not move to live in Selawik himself, his operation lasted for thirty-five years. One of his hired assistants was a man named Koen, who managed the store for the first year or so. Not much was known about Koen other than that he died in a snowstorm in the village. Another store assistant was Harry Cleveland, who later bought out Berryman around 1950.

Berryman's main competitor in the Selawik area was Louie Rotman, a fur trader who had traveled the coast as far north as Point Barrow before venturing into the Kobuk River. On the Kobuk, Rotman's routine was to make his fur collection rounds by visiting muskrat hunting camps himself and trading for the furs he wanted on the spot. For a while he served as the storekeeper for Berryman at Okok Point, a little below the present village of Kiana. Sometime between 1930 and 1935, he quit tending Berryman's store to start his own trading post along the Selawik River. His first fur enterprise on the Selawik was at Upingivik, a well-drained wooded area where he bought a cabin from a couple of mink farmers named Harry Strong and Jack Hooper who came from Nome by dog team in 1925 or 1926. This first Rotman's Store was well placed, since it was in the middle of the fur animal hunting territory and was just downriver from numerous Siilaviŋmiut upriver families living along the Kuugruaq and the Tagraġvik, the two major tributaries of the Selawik River. Prior to the establishment of Rotman's Store, upriver families had to travel all the way down to Selawik village to trade if they wanted to acquire Western goods. Rotman developed trading relationships with the local families in which the families supplied him with furs in exchange for Western commodities, a time-honored credit system that quickly led to economic dependency.

Oral accounts Douglas obtained from Arthur Skin indicated that the following families lived along the Kuugruaq River: Harry Russell, Matoolik Skin, Matoolik's brother Tommy Skin, and Ulugaaniq (a Wood from Kobuk River). Along the Tagraġvik River lived the Goodwins and the Mitchells. In the vicinity of the Upingivik on the main river lived the Kolhaks, the Davises, the Lights, and the Goodes. A little farther downriver at Niliq (Nilik) were the families of Oglu and his brother Aŋatkuq Ballot, Homer Larkin's parents, Leslie Burnette, Walter Ballot, and Johnnie Foster. These families formed the upriver demographic tapestry before the village's founding, and their descendants are present-day residents of Selawik (figure 5.1).

Figure 5.1. Ruth Ballot, oldest person in Selawik in 1971, wife of Angatkuq Ballot.

Two additional sources help provide a fuller picture of trader Louie Rotman. His first trip to Selawik was by dog team (Lee, Sampson, and Tennant 1992:167). After discovering how lucrative the fur trading there was, he decided to secure a stronger hold on the fur market by moving from Kotzebue to Upiṅġivik. According to Arthur Skin, Rotman came in later by a river transport for which he hired Arthur, who at the time was operating a freight boat between Kotzebue and the rivers. Rotman arrived in either 1930 or 1931, just before freeze-up, with his wife, Clara Levy (daughter of William Shakespeare Levy), their baby girl, Sally, and six dogs, along with one and a half cases of coffee, six cases of milk, and some tobacco that he purchased from Magids Brothers, another store in Kotzebue. The merchandise was readily purchased by the upriver families with the fur they had in their possession.

In 1932 or 1933, Rotman relocated his trading operation to Niliq, where he built a cabin and warehouse that was still standing when Douglas last visited in 2005.

Although many upriver families continued to make periodic trips down to Selawik for supplies at Berryman's trading post, the presence of Rotman's Store made Niliq the new trading center for the upriver families. There, Rotman maintained his trading post for the next three years.

An interesting character, a Greek trader named Sapolio after the soap company, moved to Niliq about the same time. Apparently Sapolio's performance of magic tricks impressed the locals immensely. One trick was swallowing a red-hot steel sword; another was taking a red-hot steel bar in his mouth and bending it. These performances prompted the upriver people to give him the Eskimo name Itnektuyit (*itnek* = fire). According to one of the Selawik elders, "The medicine men could not match his powers, so they could not kill him as they did the first miners." Sapolio spent his winters at Niliq and during the summer moved down to Selawik, where he opened another trading post from his log house. He had two Native wives and two children, Tommy Sours and Helen Kagoona. It is likely that the location of Niliq, misidentified on early USGS quadrangle maps of the area as Gabolio, is derived from his name.

In 1935, Rotman bought out his competitor Berryman's trading post in Selawik and for a time he maintained trading posts in both Niliq and Selawik. He later gave up the Niliq store operation because many upriver families were moving downriver to live in Selawik. The legacy of the Rotman trading enterprise in Selawik continues in the Rotman's Store, still in operation in Selawik as of 2023 (figure 5.2).

By the late 1930s, the bountiful supply of furs trapped throughout the valley and the inter-lakes area attracted more traders to open stores in Selawik. The Magids of Kotzebue likewise moved in, establishing their store in a log cabin that was originally the home of the Indian trade fair messenger Charlie Goodwin. The log cabin later became the headquarters of the Selawik Reindeer Company. Currently, that building has become the Seventh-day Adventist Church, which acquired the cabin from the Magids in 1950.

The second Siilaviŋmiu (plural of Siilaviŋmiut) to open a store in the village, located on Akuliġaq Island, was Aulataq (English name Walter Goode). According to Elmer Ballot, the store was a log cabin situated where the Rotman's Store is now. Goode ran his store until his death, when Hugo Eckhart, who was married to an Iñupiaq woman named Qaluuraq took over (Lee, Sampson, and Tennant 1992:163). Eckhart later left Selawik to start a fox farm on the Noatak, which did not succeed, and subsequently set up his own store in Kotzebue, which his widow operated into the 1960s.

While most of the traders mentioned above came into Selawik by way of Kotzebue, Archie Ferguson, a trader, trapper, dog musher, and freight boat captain, arrived in Selawik through kin connection. Archie was married to an Iñupiaq woman,

Figure 5.2. Rotman's Store, Selawik, 1972.

Hadley Wood (daughter of an *umialik* in Upper Kobuk), and his brother-in-law Edward Norton had settled in Selawik after the completion of the Friends Church construction contract. Archie later assigned his son Donald to manage the store. The Ferguson Store ledgers covering several years from the 1940s to 1951 (shared by Emma Norton, daughter of Edward Norton) provide an instructive picture of fur trading and a trading store operation at the time. The record gave the names of the people who sold their fur and pelts to the store. From the dates of the sale, except for the muskrats acquired during the summer months, most of other fur skins were acquired and sold to the store during the winter months, conforming to the traditional winter fur harvesting practice. It showed that in a given season a good hunter, like John Brown, could obtain as many as over a hundred muskrat skins and as many as fifteen red fox pelts for sale. The years 1947–1949 appeared to be very productive years (table 5.1).

Other fur animals purchased were red wolves at $3 to $7 per skin and fox at $12 per skin, compared to $2.25 for a muskrat skin. A wolverine ruff had a $12 value, and an otter a $25 value. The highest prices went for mink pelts, varying from $8 per skin in 1943 to as much as $45 in 1948. To transport the furs from Selawik to Kotzebue, the Fergusons had their own freight boat. From Kotzebue, the Fergusons sent their furs out to the Seattle Fur Exchange Company.

Following the usual practice, Archie Ferguson used the credit system to acquire the furs. The amount of cash Natives earned for the fur sales was held as a balance or as fur credit against the purchased commodities. These included food products, particularly coffee, tea, pilot bread, salt, flour, and lard; other household items used

TABLE 5.1. Fur harvest of Selawik trappers sold to Ferguson Store compiled by Wanni Anderson from the Ferguson Store Ledgers.

Time period	Mink	Weasel	Red fox	Beaver	Lynx	Otter	Marten	Muskrat
Winter 1947	121	14	23					
Winter 1948	97	89	15	20	2	1	0	105
Winter and summer 1949	91	89	4	24	3	5	10	2,834

in the household; tobacco; and merchandise such as tents, boat gasoline, lanterns, matches, knives, axes, kettles, ropes, saws, flashlights, and dog chains. Personal included toothbrushes, combs, eyeglasses, shirts, pants, overalls, socks, muslin cloth, calico, blankets, mittens, soap, aspirin and other medicine, and castor oil. Earnings from Native labor for the store such as longshoring and cutting cords of firewood were also held as credits for store merchandise (Rotman's Store 1940–1942).

The ledgers provide interesting insights into the entire credit system in Selawik. Residents occasionally requested that their own earned credits be donated to the general account of the Friends Church. Also, requests were made to lend store credit to friends, thereby making the store a semi-banking enterprise that still functions at present in villages of the region without a bank.

In 1929, Ferguson started a fur farm, raising mink and later also marten. He also erected a sawmill whose remnants were still to be seen in the 1970s. The mill was first constructed and operated in the Upper Kobuk but was later sledded over to Selawik by an impressive team of 100 dogs. A major village construction project in which the new technology put to use was the Seventh-day Adventist Church's renovations of its original log cabin into a timber construction. The lumber processed at the mill used for the construction of the church was from logs floated down to Selawik from Purcell Mountain.

Somewhat later, another store, in operation for only a short while, opened in Selawik. It was owned by Robinson Blankenship, whose main store, still in operation today, is in Kiana. Blankenship and Ferguson were strong competitors until Blankenship decided to give up his Selawik branch.

By the late 1940s, Selawik business community was marked by four trading posts operating side by side: Berryman's, Rotman's, Ferguson's, and Magids'. The Ferguson fur farm, initially profitable, unfortunately failed at a later date. The Selawik fur trading boom, like reindeer herding, became a part of Selawik history.

Elder Ralph Ramoth attributed the presence of numerous trading posts in Selawik to the heavy competition among the region's fur traders during the period of high fur prices. The purchase of fur and pelts from Ferguson's (see table 5.1)

Figure 5.3. One of the abandoned freight boats, possibly the Ferguson boat (center right), that once plied the Selawik to Kotzebue waterways (D. Anderson photo, 1971).

was from only one trading post. While no record is available for the total purchase from the four trading posts in the village, it could be said that during the 1930s and 1940s, Selawik was in its prosperous heyday as the commercial center of the region, visually represented by three old, abandoned freight boats, formerly owned by traders plying the river, that were still part of the village landscape in the 1970s (figure 5.3).

The history of fur trading and the early trading stores in Selawik is a story about two groups of entrepreneurs. The first group was the local Iñupiaq traders like Matoolik and Walter Goode, who carried on the goods exchange tradition of the past into the modern time with a new type of merchandise, Western goods. The second group was the adventurous *nalaumi* (white men) who pursued their uncharted routes into remote Alaskan territories. Many in the latter group came as traders or prospectors from far beyond Alaska. Others wandered in from earlier ventures in Alaska, first to Kotzebue and then to the more remote villages. Some married Iñupiaq women and settled in to become fully integrated into the Iñupiaq world. As village traders, they could be regarded as cultural agents who introduced Western material culture, commodities, food items, and technologies from sawmills to outboard motors and snowmachines. They could be said to be conduits of the cash economy in the village. On the Selawik River, in addition to Sapolio (called Inektuyit), others were given Iñupiaq names by locals. Hugo Eckhart was called Yuukuuraq, while Archie Ferguson's parents were referred to on the Kobuk as Fergusialutku and Aaŋŋapaurraat. Robinson Blankenship was called Pliagruaq

(Lee, Sampson, and Tennant 1992:17,163). These Iñupiaq names, which incorporated them into the Iñupiaq social world, attest to their significant roles and relationships in the communities.

The major drawback of an overreliance on furs as the basis of the Selawik economy was that trapping was not a dependable source of income. As a component
of the international fur economy, prices and demand fluctuated greatly (Jenness
1962:15). Combined with the practice of the credit system of the trading posts, this
often left Selawik families with unsustainable debt. Trading post owners were frequently forced to dissolve the debt or risk losing their customers.

6

Introduction of Reindeer Herding

A US government program, begun the same year as the founding of the Selawik school and church in 1908, had a profound impact on the Siilaviŋmiut. This was the introduction of reindeer herding into Selawik.

Nineteen years earlier, in 1891, Sheldon Jackson had introduced the practice of reindeer herding into Alaska to alleviate the supposed food shortages brought about by the decline of caribou and sea mammals in the region (US Bureau of Education 1908). After a slow start on Seward Peninsula, the project gained in popularity, and within a few years the number of reindeer began to increase dramatically. The initial problem was that the first domesticated reindeer had been imported from the Siberian Chukchi, with whom Eskimos and government supervisors had issues. But after three years, in 1894, the federal government began to import more cooperative Lapp reindeer herders and their families—and, later, also reindeer—from Norway. Jackson's far-reaching humanitarian plan was originally designed to establish a few central breeding stations to which Native apprentices would be admitted for training and then acquire loaner deer to start their own herds. The government also lent reindeer for starter herds to some missions and even to the Lapp teachers. It was soon realized that the scheme, although somewhat successful, did not distribute reindeer to the local Natives quickly enough to achieve its original aims (Postell 1990). As a result, by 1900 the plans were revised to establish numerous smaller reindeer stations, each with its own apprenticeship program administered by local officials. Since representatives of the missionary societies were already on

https://doi.org/10.5876/9781646426065.c006

hand in the coastal villages, local missionaries/teachers were tasked with that job as well. And, continuing with the then-established protocols, the missions were also loaned their own small starter herds to manage alongside the government herds. By this time, the possibilities of reindeer herding must have been well-known to the Selawik families, although the distribution of starter herds was primarily administered through the missionaries in the coastal villages such as Kotzebue.

The revised plan was soon considered ineffective as well, and by 1908 several new modifications were made to the apprentice system (Olsen 1969:38). The missions were no longer in charge of distributing reindeer to the Natives. Instead, individual Natives were able to acquire their starter herds directly from the government, or even from other Native or Lapp deer owners, without having to go through the missions. Despite private ownership by Natives, however, the US Board of Education (Stern et al. 1980:36) required the government teachers/missionaries in the villages to monitor the Native herds, a practice that continued the role of the teachers/missionary as a major influence in Native affairs.

This was the state of the reindeer program when, in 1908, a few Selawik families got involved. Although there are few records detailing the introduction of the reindeer into Selawik, we have been able to glean its history from school reports by teachers who were local government representatives of the reindeer program (US Department of Education reports for 1910–1914, 1916, and 1919), missionary reports to the California Yearly Meeting (Friends) for 1897–1955, and former Selawik reindeer herders, especially Richard Jones, William Sheldon, and Andrew Skin. In an interview, Jones, who was nineteen years old in 1908, described his experiences as follows:

> I first heard about reindeer herding on one of my annual seal hunting trips to Kotzebue. Then in 1908 when I was visiting Candle I learned about the reindeer program in detail from government representatives. It seemed that the reindeer that had been introduced to Wales village [the large village at the easternmost tip of Seward Peninsula] several years earlier had expanded to the point that several new government herds were being started and moved to different parts of interior Seward Peninsula.
>
> That same year Mr. Evans, sent word to the people of Selawik that under the new regulations of the government's reindeer program some of these animals were now available for acquisition by individual Natives. Several Selawik men including me took up the inducement. After breakup we carried a boat over the isthmus of Baldwin Peninsula to Kotzebue Sound and sailed to Candle to see about acquiring some reindeer. We were eventually able to acquire a loan of 150 reindeer from one of the Mary's Igloo herds which, along with 35 deer for a Sisualik herdsman, 100 for the Laplander

Nelliman and 75 for Kotzebue herder Oglivaluk, we were able to drive the herds over to them. (D. Anderson interview with Richard Jones, Selawik, October 27, 1971)

Additional information from governmental correspondence supplements Jones's account, though citing a different number of reindeer involved. According to a letter from William Hamilton, acting chief of the Alaska Division, Bureau of Education, to Michael White, captain of the sailing vessel *Volante*, on December 23, 1908, 100 reindeer scheduled for Selawik were sent by ship to Kotzebue. It thus appears that the herd to be driven to Selawik was picked up in Kotzebue.

Under the tutelage of Oglivaluk, an important Native herd owner from Kotzebue who also grazed some of his own deer with the Selawik herd, the hardworking Selawik men quickly became skilled herders. Their herd grew rapidly. The number of deer listed for Selawik in 1909 was 322, which must have included those belonging to Oglivaluk. In 1910, the herd increased to 448. By 1911, the government had the Selawik herders sent seventy-five deer to Buckland to add to a large herd that was being started there (figure 6.1).

The reindeer program was highly popular from the beginning. According to the School Report of 1913:

> The natives of Selawik are much interested in the deer. Many of them have purchased deer. . . . The people of the village try to put all their extra money into deer and the old herders never want to sell females unless they are forced to. Both show the serious manner in which these people have taken up the industry.

The positive momentum of the program can be seen in a 1918 record. Selawik was able to maintain two separate herds and was even able to send 800 deer to Shungnak on the Kobuk River.

That period was indeed a time of high optimism for the entire Iñupiaq reindeer project—one further heightened by the introduction of the government's annual reindeer fair in 1915 designed to promote herding activities in the region. The fairs were popular among the herders, including the Selawik herdsmen who enthusiastically joined in all of the program's activities. The first fair in Northwest Alaska was held at Mary's Igloo on the Seward Peninsula (VanStone, Kakaru, and Lucier 2000). In the winter of 1915–1916, one of the fairs took place at Noorvik.

We do not know if any Selawik herders attended the first fair. But in the second round of the fairs, held at Kruszgamepa Hot Springs, north of Nome and at Noorvik, it was highly likely that Selawik herders participated, especially at Noorvik. Selawik herders definitely participated in the third round of fairs, held at Noatak. Selawik teacher Frank M. Jones provided an account in *The Eskimo Magazine*, a small local publication he started with Evans. The fourth annual

Figure 6.1. A reindeer herder and animal from Northwest Alaska (photograph from *National Geographic*, December 1919).

fair was scheduled for 1918 in Noatak, but it is not clear whether it actually happened. The worldwide influenza epidemic of 1918 took the lives of several of the major herders, including Walter C. Shields, superintendent for education for the Northwestern District of Alaska, the original organizer of the fairs. This epidemic, which also decimated many of the Iñupiaq families on Seward Peninsula, put an end to the fairs, never to be revived.

In Selawik, however, strict quarantine measures adopted by village leaders barring people from traveling to market their whitefish and reindeer meat, had largely spared the population from the flu. Here, life in the village and the reindeer camps largely continued as usual.

The herds and their grazing ranges continued to grow—so much so that by the early 1920s, it was becoming difficult for herders to keep individual herds apart. From a proposal initiated by the Department of Agriculture to reorganize herds as cooperatives, Selawik herders decided to consolidate their herds into a single company called the Selawik Reindeer and Trading Company. Incorporated on April 16, 1925, it operated as a joint stock company with shares to be purchased at $20 per share. A person could purchase a share with cash or purchase a reindeer at the rate of one deer per share. The company was governed by nine board members: Lester Young, Harry Cleveland, Ikik Sheldon, Pupik Harrison, Albert Skin, Peter Goode, Jimmie Foster, Henry Jackson, and the resident BIA schoolteacher, Walter Nichols. The original membership consisted of forty-two Selawik residents, including the Selawik Eskimo Friends Church, which was granted also the right to own reindeer.

At the peak of reindeer herding in the mid-1930s, nearly all Selawik families were heavily involved in the enterprise. Reindeer herding was the main economic lifeway. The Selawik Reindeer Company had three different herds, numbering 26,000 head: one managed by Jimmy Foster and his brothers; another by Richard Jones, who had the largest herd; and a third by Charlie Smith. Each shareholder could cash in a share, that is, request a reindeer to be butchered for them at any time, a practice that later led to difficulties for the entire enterprise. By 1936, the ownerships were distributed among 148 shareholders, or more than half of the population of Selawik. Only two families did not own any reindeer.

As if by coincidence, the very next fall Selawik herders, as well as herders from other parts of Northwest Alaska, began to experience problems—the loss of their reindeer. In 1937, the number of reindeer in the Selawik herd was said to have been reduced from 26,000 to 10,537. According to a Department of the Interior Reindeer Service circular dated March 15, 1937, a major problem was predation by wolves. "In the past two years wolves have killed thousands of reindeer from the Selawik, Noorvik, Kivalina, and other herds. They have almost destroyed the Selawik herd."

Other experts offered different reasons for the decline. Some argued that the problem was the inadequate herding skills of herders. Others attributed it to the commercialization of the reindeer industry, which was in full swing and led to an oversupply of animals and overgrazing. Reindeer herder Richard Jones attributed the decline not to mismanagement but to a changed ecological condition, possibly overgrazing coupled with several years of especially severe weather conditions in winter and spring. Jones also told Douglas that the herding techniques they had been taught were no longer adequate for coping with new circumstances. He attributed the failure to multiple interconnected causes rather than to a single cause.

Selawik herders operating in the 1950s and 1960s who were interviewed cited animal behavior as an additional explanation. They argued that the problem was caused by the deer running off with caribou, which were then increasing in numbers throughout Northwest Alaska. Before the increase of the caribou, reindeer could be left by themselves at night and during summer to spread out and graze on their own. This loose herding method could be carried out by foot and with dogs. The herder needed only to make a round in a big circle around the band each day without disturbing it, other than working in the few strays that wandered too far afield. But as the caribou population increased, the reindeer started straying. As a result, herds had to be closely supervised, a task that required more manpower and a constant twenty-four-hour daily attention. Herder Ray Skin's diary of day-to day-activities in the summer of 1942 is illustrative of the hard work herders had to put in to keep their herds together. Evident from his account is that the herders had to be constantly on the move, chasing down straying deer and bringing them back to the main herd:

> *8-15-41 Saturday*: Today we are still pushing the herd. There are many that are unmarked. The fawns are unmarked. They killed one fawn for their food. We met manager Chas Smith.

> *8-16-42 Sunday*: We still are punching up the unmarked reindeer. Our manager brought us Kar-beck and some dried fish. Roy and Sam came to us today. They bring us some fawn meat from which they killed. We slept here at Kar-ly-vik Lake. Our herd is scattered all over.

> *8-17-42 Monday*: Sam, Ed and Roy are walking and Chas and I by kayak. We punchered [*sic*] and pushed the herd down the river. Today we travel here to No-yaot-t, and An-na-cock Ballot's fish camp. We used some white grub and seal oil from his stuff, then we left one fawn skin to him.

> *8-18-42 Tuesday*: Today we travel again with lots of punches and pushing. We slept near Era-jer-seevik. At noon we punched one. This evening, Chas killed one crippled fawn because we were out of food. We saved the skin.

By 1943, the Selawik Reindeer and Trading Company's herd had declined to fewer than 3,000 head. At the same time, Selawik residents were also experiencing shortages of fish and other wild animals due in part to several particularly harsh winter and spring seasons. To address the food shortage, the families cashed in 233 of their shares. The next year, 301 animals were butchered, and an additional 461 animals were lost through other causes, including wolf predation. In 1945, the herd was down to 2,000 head, and by 1949 down to 1,500 head. Apparently, with the share system of one deer per share still in effect, families were calling in their shares at a rate that made it practically impossible for the herd to replenish itself.

The Reindeer Company was unfortunately too slow to recognize the incompatibility of this share system with a declining herd. As a result, the Selawik Reindeer Company (apparently dropping the word "Trading" in its title) decided on a different approach: they loaned the entire herd to herder Charlie Smith to see if he could reverse the trend. At the time of the loan, only 500 reindeer remained.

In this private ownership system, modeled after that of the Laplanders, Charlie's herd had several successful years, including being able in 1954 to send 600 pounds of reindeer meat to Point Barrow.

In the 1950s, several other Selawik men, encouraged by Charlie Smith's success, ventured to start their own herds by borrowing the reindeer from the government herd at Escholtz Bay. But by 1959, only two Selawik herders were listed in the village census: William Sheldon (Ikik's son) and Andrew Skin (Matoolik's son). According to Sheldon, so many caribou came by and more reindeer ran away with them that he could not keep the herd steady. In 1962, the supervisor informed Sheldon that he could get another starter herd, but Sheldon declined the offer, rationalizing that when the caribou herd migrated the next year, he would have the same problem. He added in his interview with Douglas that this was the reason that the Noatak, Kivalina, and Kobuk herders had all given up.

By the 1970s, the reindeer herding era of Selawik was a faint memory in all but the last of the surviving herders. The only visible reminder of this engrossing economic history is the original building of the Selawik Reindeer Company (formerly the home of the Selawik Indian trade fair messenger Charlie Goodwin), now the Seventh-day Adventist Church.

PART 2

Through the Ethnographic Lens

Selawik from the 1970s

7

The Long, Cold Winter

[H]uman existence is irrevocably situated in time and space . . .
—KEITH H. BASSO (1996:53)

Like their Iñupiaq neighbors, Siilaviŋmiut conceived the annual seasonal cycle as two basic seasons: winter (*ukiuk*), the period of closed water, and summer (*upiṅaaq*), the period of open water, modified by suffixes to identify times of moving into or coming out of the core seasons.

In late August, foliage began to change color. Leaves of birch and willow trees turned golden yellow and the tundra vegetation myriad gorgeous shades of red. One sensed the coming of dark nights, somewhat unsettling after the long, pleasant sunny days of summer. Days got perceptibly shorter, losing the bright daylight at four minutes a clip. But, thankfully, the mosquito swarms began to drop off. It was now fall (*ukiaksraq*). As the Iñupiaq word expressed, it was becoming winter.

Forewarned by the coming of the season of closed water, Selawik families redoubled their fishing efforts. In the cooler, drier weather of fall, fish, even the fatty sheefish, could be hung to dry without the worry of spoiling. It was an opportune time for families to try to increase their supply of dry fish for the approaching winter on top of what they had accumulated during the summer.

By mid-August, the small whitefish called *ikkuiyiq* (*Prosopium cylindraceum*) were especially abundant on the Fish River, a small but important stream flowing into the lake area north of the Selawik River. Families whose ancestral homes were in this area

https://doi.org/10.5876/9781646426065.c007

boated from Selawik through lakes and sloughs to their old river-edge home allotment sites to seine for whitefish and burbot. Many set up their fish-drying racks to dry the fish before transporting them back to the village; others brought their catch back to dry in the village. Some women set up gill nets at their own traditional netting stations to catch whitefish, pike, and, if they could, the big sheefish.

Fall was also the prime season for hunters to come across wandering moose. Moose, which had begun to appear in the region in the 1920s, had increased by the 1970s and 1980s to the extent that they were an additional, important meat resource for Selawik residents. A few hunters, hungry for fresh meat after a summer of fish, occasionally started to hunt even before the official opening of the moose hunting season, which in 1970 was August 20. Once the hunting season opened, most hunters set out eagerly. Moose hunting season was brief, not simply because of the game laws but also because hunters wanted to harvest the game before the rutting season that peaked in mid- to late September, which would make the male moose meat stink. The best moose hunting areas around Selawik were upriver, where the animals could be reached by boat. Once a moose was brought down near the river's edge, its heavy carcass could be easily hauled back to the village. That the moose was a relatively recent introduction to the region was attested by the fact that most Selawik women did not make use of their skins. Only those who had an Indian background reportedly knew how to tan the thick hides, and even these few women did not bother.

Selawik residents' sense of fall included opportunities to hunt ducks and geese. The lakes and sloughs of the Selawik basin were important waterfowl nesting areas, where many of the species assembled in large flocks before starting their long migrations southward. Duck hunting, important to augment the diet, increased throughout August and September. Most men went out to hunt in either evenings or early mornings. Many combined their hunting activity with their wives' net-checking trips. While out there, hunters were also on the lookout for the caribou, which were then just beginning to migrate through. By early October, the caribou herds migrating from the North Slope to Seward Peninsular began to appear in increasing numbers, with 100–300 caribou at a time moving southward through the lower Selawik and inter-lake areas. Other herds migrated through the upriver areas, particularly along the Kuugruaq and Tagraġvik valleys. Caribou is the quintessential game animal for the Siilaviŋmiut, as it is for all riverine and interior Iñupiat. They are the source of not only their meat supply, nowadays supplemented by the moose meat, but also of other products. Caribou skin, antler, and bones are materials for making clothing and manufacturing tools. The caribou hunting skills of Iñupiaq men and the skin sewing skills of Iñupiaq women are legendary. Even in the twenty-first century, these skills continue largely undiminished.

Figure 7.1. Enclosed platform caches in Selawik.

With freeze-up soon to arrive, activities that required travel by open water became a foremost concern. Families began transporting in the last of their dried fish from their fish camps to their enclosed platform caches in the village (figure 7.1).

Women were likewise busy refitting their fish nets for the winter fishing. The nets were tied with heavier sinkers, necessary to keep the nets safely submerged below the ice. The nets were piled in front of their homes, ready to be hauled out to their winter ice netting locations. Some families readied these locations by sinking ropes between stakes across sloughs where the under-ice nets could be strung after freeze-up. Men pulled their boats and motors onto the shore to safely store them for the approaching winter, generally setting the boats bottoms-up to keep out the winter snow.

If logs needed for house building or repair were to be rafted downriver or across the Selawik Lake to the village, it had to be accomplished quickly. To be caught on the river or lake with the ice forming meant losing the logs they had acquired through backbreaking work. They might even lose the chance to get back home before the ice was frozen in the Selawik River.

When we spent the 1971–1972 winter in Selawik, the end of September or early October saw the last barge coming in from Kotzebue carrying building supplies and the crucial load of fifty-five-gallon drums of fuel oil. When the barge arrived, it was all hands on deck, as men and strong older boys unloaded the drums, rolling them from the barge to the shore along narrow gangplanks. Longshoring provided a welcome source of income, especially for the boys, who had few other opportunities to earn money.

In October, freeze-up on the Selawik River ushered in cold, winter days and long nights. The Selawik River did not freeze overnight, however. For a person whose livelihood was not connected to an Arctic river, the gradual process of a river freeze-up and witnessing what happened to a once lively, navigable wide expanse of water could be a bewildering experience. In 1971, we had the first snow at the end of September. Thin ice sheets began to form on top of the river, and that sent a warning. Outboard motorboats that used to navigate up and down the river gradually suspended their activities as people began to walk gingerly on the ice at the water's edge when they needed to haul up water from the river. They carefully listened to cracking sounds as they walked over the fresh ice. Crashing through the ice was not a comforting thought, as many had been known to have died by accidental drowning through thin ice. We once witnessed three careless young people on a snowmobile crash through the soft river ice—they escaped a soaking but lost their machine. A school student reported that week's big event in her class essay, "The snowmobile was drown!"

Even after early October, when the river ice cover became permanent, rising temperatures could open up "slush soft spots" or even holes in the ice. People avoided the hazardous spots by marking them with willow branches or empty Clorox bottles. Before the building of the bridges from the school side of the river to the island and from the island to the airport side of the river, which occurred several years after our year there, it was unsafe for students to try to cross over to school at this time. Those who did not live on the school side were excused from classes until the river was frozen solid and they could walk safely across. People tuned in on their CB radios to hear who would be the first brave person to successfully walk or ride their snowmobile across the river. The news was passed on, and the winter traffic on the frozen Selawik River commenced. Our sense of the coming of the Selawik winter was heightened one day by an exciting sight of a blurry figure of a dog-team driver whipping by through the light snow downriver.

With the arrival of winter, the region morphed into a white world where river, lake, and terrain merged into a single vast, white landscape. In the village, the Selawik River turned into a solid pathway connecting the island and both sides of the river. The constant traffic of people crossing the river everywhere and at any time became a new pattern of life in the village. Kids began ice skating on the river close to the shore (figure 7.2).

Even small children who were still unsteady ice skaters joined in to welcome the winter. Some pushed outboard motor covers turned upside down, simulating driving a sled, or showed up in home-made wooden miniature sleds, pulled by an older brother, if not by an excited puppy (figure 7.3).

The rhythm of winter was punctuated by frequent sights of hooded hunters on the frozen river leaving the village on their snowmobiles, towing basket sleds to

Figure 7.2. Children ice skating on the frozen Selawik River early in the winter season, 1971.

Figure 7.3. Children trying out their first "dog team."

look for herds of caribou migrating nearby (figure 7.4). A successful hunter could bring back a sled load, as many as five caribou at a time, while stashing the rest of his hunt to be recovered on later trips. Although most hunters hunted by snowmobile, a few older hunters continued to use their dog teams (figure 7.5).

Although by 1970 nearly all families owned snowmobiles, many retained their dogs staked out by their houses, ready to be hitched up again if they ran out of money for gas (figure 7.6). Maintaining a dog team, while labor-intensive with the need for a lot of fish as dog feed, offered a hunting flexibility for these families.

When not hunting, some men traveled to Fish River to construct a fish weir, if they had not already done so during fall. If they used a dog team as their travel mode, they could arrive there right after freeze-up, since the dogsled's lighter means of transport enabled them to navigate the thin river ice well before others could arrive on heavier snowmobiles. The weir, made of spruce and willow poles, covered by a five-foot-deep chicken wire fence, functioned as a porous dam across the river with an opening for a dip net (figure 7.7). Fish-weir fishing was mostly a men's activity.

The U-shaped dip net for fish weirs was designed specifically for scooping down to the shallow river bottom. A two-man team was required to scoop the fish out. In the early 1970s, their catch was prolific, as Douglas witnessed them heaping pile after pile of fish on the shore to freeze, to be retrieved later in the season. Besides the countless whitefish (*ikkuiyiq*), they were able to scoop up hundreds of the bottom-feeding burbot.

Women's fishing activities continued in a different form during the cold winter months. As soon as the ice was sufficiently solid, women began to set their winter nets. Those who had earlier strung their net lines before the ice formed were able to quickly ply the nets out by attaching them to ropes and pulling them under the ice (figure 7.8). Those who had not prepared the site had to string the nets under the ice by chopping a line of holes through to push it along. Women continued to use these nets as long as they could be pulled up. Later in winter, when the ice thickened to the point of incorporating the tops of the nets, the nets would be frozen in, not retrievable until spring. This signaled the end of the net ice fishing season.

Another method of winter fishing was ice-hole hooking called *niksiksuq*. Men traveled to Selawik Lake to hook for sheefish. Ice fishing was especially productive in the early winter. The primary device was a short L-shaped pole to which a fish-shaped hook characteristic of the Selawik and Kobuk River Iñupiat was attached (figure 7.9).

A number of Selawik men of the older generation were skilled fish-hook makers, and among the most prolific was Walter Ballot, who donated numerous to our collection (figure 7.10). Among this collection are fish hooks that incorporate Western materials, such as two aluminum sheefish hooks (k, l) cast from melted World War II water canteens with holes drilled for the insertion of colored plastic

Figure 7.4. A pair of hunters on frozen Selawik River on their way to the hunt.

Figure 7.5. Returning from the hunt by dog team.

Figure 7.6. Dogs staked out as back-up transportation.

Figure 7.7. Fishing by dip net at a Fish River weir.

Figure 7.8. Lenora and Arthur Skin working together at ice fishing.

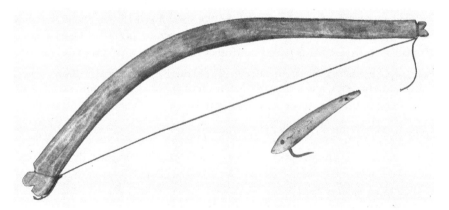

Figure 7.9. An ice fishing pole and fish-lure hook designed for sheefishing. The fish-shaped hook is made of walrus ivory, and its green eyes are made from a plastic toothbrush handle.

for fish eyes. Walter also made a sheefish-lure hook (b) and a burbot hook (a) from an arm of a weighing scale. Fish-hook craftsmen also made smaller versions of fish-lure hooks for pike and grayling (m, o, and possibly i).

A good half-day of ice-hole fishing could land as many as twenty to forty large sheefish, which would be immediately frozen in the frigid winter temperatures as low as −35 degrees Fahrenheit during the daytime (figure 7.11). The caught fish could be stacked on the sled like cordwood for transporting back to the village. Warm sheefish soup was a healthy, welcoming dish during the frigid winter.

During winter, men, women, and children also set snares, often just beyond the edge of town. Ptarmigans and rabbits were especially important as supplementary fresh meat for their diet before the caribou migrated over.

Some men also began to trap early in the winter, especially if the family needed fox skins as ruff trimmings for their winter parkas. But most waited until after Christmas, when the furs of the fur-bearing animals were at their longest and thickest. For decades, these prime late-winter or early-spring pelts, especially fox and mink, provided desirable sources of income for Selawik families. In the last few decades of the twentieth century, however, fur prices on the world market became so volatile that devoting much time to trapping was often a gamble.

Muskrat and beaver hunting commenced in early spring. In the lower Selawik area, some hunters managed to get as many as a hundred muskrats a night, using .22 rifles. Muskrat furs were popular for parkas among the Iñupiat throughout Northwest Alaska, with individually designed parka styles and trimmings a matter of pride among Iñupiaq seamstresses. Men's parkas were usually made from the darker muskrat back furs. A common women's style was made of lighter muskrat belly parts (figure 7.12).

The muskrat population began to decline in the 1970s. Local trappers attributed the decline to the increase of the beaver population and their damming and flooding of the muskrat denning sites. In the 1980s, muskrat hunting was reinvigorated, this time primarily for the commercial sale of the skins to the local Rotman's Store in the village or at a higher price to the Rotman's Store in Kotzebue. By this period, Selawikers preferred to wear the washable, store-bought parka, easier to take care of in their more modern life.

Beaver skins were also desirable since the beaver strips added decoration and warmth to the winter muskrat parka. In the 1970s, the increase of beavers in the area was considered a mixed blessing. Not only did the beaver dams adversely affect the muskrat population, they also blocked stream and lake outlets, thereby impeding the fish migration patterns.

Winter was a good season to travel. Selawik residents frequently traveled to nearby villages, particularly those along the next river, the Kobuk River. With the introduction of snowmobiles, inter-village trips that formerly had taken a whole day by dog

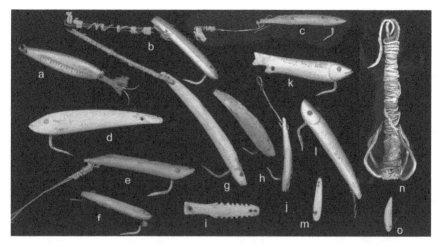

Figure 7.10. Fish hooks made by Selawik craftsmen: burbot hooks (a, n); sheefish hooks (b–h, j–l); pike (?) hook (i); grayling hooks (m, n).

Figure 7.11. Arthur Skin ice fishing for shee at Selawik Lake.

Figure 7.12. Muskrat fur parkas (left, back fur parka; right, belly fur parka).

team could be accomplished in just two to three hours. This was not only due to the faster speed of the snowmobiles. When dog teams were used, the travel routes were often circuitous, as travelers needed to find low banks for crossing the streams and lakeshores. A snowmobile, by contrast, could navigate all but the steepest banks, so their routes could be more direct. Traveling in winter by snowmobile to Kobuk villages was likewise shorter and more direct than going by boat during the summer, since the latter involved having to boat through Selawik Lake and Kotzebue Sound before entering the Kobuk River. Selawikers had numerous relatives in Kobuk villages and were fond of visiting them whenever they could. The main impediment to more frequent travel was the need to stay home and keep the children in school.

SELAWIK HALLOWEEN AND THANKSGIVING

Three major village celebrations brightened the darkness of winter: Halloween, Thanksgiving, and Christmas. As elsewhere, Halloween in Selawik was a period of fun for children. Parents made ghostly costumes for them and village stores ordered

Figure 7.13. Andersons' house in winter of 1971–1972.

in masks to sell. Our house at the end of the village, across a creek from the village cemetery, provided a good, spooky atmosphere for trick-or-treaters (figure 7.13). Many children braved the snow and knocked on our door. We ran out of candies in a hurry and had to quickly make popcorn balls as backup.

Adults and children alike eagerly anticipated the coming of Thanksgiving and Christmas, with the families celebrating them together as fun and happy community events. The account of the two feasts in winter 1970 shows how the Christian religious celebrations and the Iñupiaq feasting and celebratory traditions merged to become uniquely Selawik Iñupiaq celebrations.

Thanksgiving Day started off in the morning with a local six-dog team race. Spectators cheered on their favorite team as the route passed from the main channel in front of the school house, south around the island, and back to the starting point. In 1970, Charlie Mitchell came in first and Grant Ballot second. The winning racers, with a time of a little over an hour, received no prize except recognition. The racers did not mind. It was the fun of the race, the opportunity to give the dogs a good exercise run, and the strengthened community spirit that counted. Strong, excited dogs did not want to quit running at the finish line and had to be held back.

The Seventh-day Adventist Church, located on the school side of the river, held a small Thanksgiving party for its congregation first, in the afternoon. Although the church canons prescribed a non-meat diet, it was not possible for the pastor, Mike Schwartz, and his wife, Carole, to function in the Selawik setting without incorporating meat into their feast to a certain extent. For the twenty-three church members at the party, caribou soup mixed with spaghetti was served with potato salad, fruit Jell-O, chocolate cake, cupcakes, and green-and-orange popcorn balls made especially for children.

Later that day, a bigger communal Thanksgiving feast took place for the entire village in the Friends Church on the island. The wooden pews had been rearranged the day before to accommodate the entire village. Early in the afternoon, runners went around on snowmobiles and sleds to each house to collect the foods that families had prepared for the feast. The program chairperson received the foods and recorded the names of each donor as the runners arrived back with the load. Foods included large pots of caribou soup, dried fish, ingredients for fruit punch, cases of canned fruit, and pilot bread. Douglas joined the church volunteers to make gallons of Kool-Aid mixed with Tang while other volunteers set up other foods to be served.

The one-room church was packed with about 200 people sitting in family groups of parents and children. They arrived with paper bags and cartons containing their own bowls, soup spoons, and containers for taking home extra food. The program started with a committee member listing the food gifts, giving the name and amount of each donor. The first food donation announced was a caribou that was made into the soup, donated by "young hunter," the title accorded to a young hunter when he got his first caribou. "One whole caribou given by the young hunter Gary Smith." Everyone cheered and clapped their hands. The first caribou is the iconic game animal for an Iñupiaq hunter's rite of passage, and the occasion is celebrated and the hunter honored. By tradition, the hunting donation was the first to be honored in the announcement.

The church emcee then announced the first course to be served, dried fish. Servers went down the aisles handing everyone a couple of sections of dried fish. They came around again and again, handing out more and more until all was gone. Everyone ate one or two sections and put the rest in the bags or a carton they had brought with them.

Next came the caribou soup. The announcement elicited a loud, anticipating "ooh" from the children. Everyone got out their bowl and spoon. The servers came around again, one server to a paired row, and dished out the soup. The serving spoons used for the occasion were the Iñupiaq traditional large hand-carved wooden dippers called the *qalutauraq*, which worked better than commercial spoons. Each dipperful could fill a large bowl. Servers dished out more on the second round until the pot was finished. Then the serving of another pot of caribou soup was announced, with name of the donor. This was followed yet with another pot of caribou soup, until all soup had been served. Each pot of soup had been prepared differently, one with rice, another with macaroni, and a third with canned tomatoes. These are Iñupiaq fusion cuisine.

Figure 7.14. Esther Outwater (right) with her twin sister Gladys Downey of Ambler, who came to Selawik for the spring carnival, 1972.

The dessert course followed. Cupcakes were first served to expectant children and olives to adults. Pilot bread, a staple of Alaska bush life, was the next item on the menu. At least twenty cases of pilot bread gifts were stacked on the platform. The pilot bread was distributed four to six pieces at a time. As servers came up and down the aisles, each family put their handfuls in their bags or carton to be stored for the next meal at home. Eventually, each person received about a carton's worth. Children were also given bubblegum to take home. Canned fruits were served as the last course.

Finally, with a closing prayer, the feast was over. The families happily returned home, loaded with enough food to last for days.

SELAWIK CHRISTMAS AND THE NEW YEAR WEEK

Christmas presented another occasion for villagers to celebrate as a community. The conviviality started a few days before Christmas Day. On December 23, 1971, while men had fun together at the men-only dart game in the Community Hall, the Selawik Mothers' Club organized their own get-together, to which Wanni was invited. Nancy Starbuck and Esther Outwater (figure 7.14) were co-organizers. After a prayer, several parlor games, including animal pantomimes and a chocolate-bar-eating contest, were enjoyed, with a lot of laughs, followed by a small gift exchange. Cake and Jell-O were served with Kool-Aid as the refreshment.

As at Thanksgiving, the big Christmas community feast took place in the Friends Church with about 300 adults and children. The program, printed on a mimeographed sheet, began with the children's performance, each saying "their piece," a short six- to twenty-word recitation. They were rewarded with applause. Candy was distributed, accompanied by the announcement of the donors' names. After the sharing of Christmas dinner like at Thanksgiving, gifts were given. The gifts festooned the front of the church. Several volunteers handed them out to the persons named—to children from parents, from a relative to another relative, from a friend to another friend. A unique Iñupiaq cultural tradition incorporated into the Christian celebration was the giving of thank-you gifts to individuals who had helped with the funeral preparations during the year from the family of the deceased. The event continued until past midnight.

The most exciting Iñupiaq activity was the five-day Eskimo Games that took place in the evenings in the armory building from December 25 to 30.

On the first night, about fifty or sixty people were present, mainly older teenagers and young adults. The contestants were organized into two teams. A person who arrived late could choose any side they wished to join. In addition to games of skill and dexterity, there were games of strength or tenacity in the face of pain, a cultivation of physical toughness and endurance. In Selawik in 1970–1971, there were twenty-two different games, none of which was repeated the following days:

1. Pulling two loops on a short rope with the little finger of the right hand.
2. Pulling two 1.5-inch-round sticks tied with a three-to-four-inch rope with little fingers of both hands. Two other players pass a string over the top of the joining string and at right angle hold the sticks down.
3. Jumping over a stick with a loop of rope around the neck. The loop was shortened by a half hitch each round.
4. Jumping over a stick tied to a rope that hung from a beam overhead. The rope was passed under the legs and back up.
5. Leg wrestle, beginning with hooked left ankles and hooked left elbow.
6. Arm pulling
7. Looped string pulling with nose.
8. Pulling oneself up on two ropes until the arms were straight and then hooked around knees. Starting from the sitting position.
9. Distance jumping over a pole.
10. Distance jumping starting backward.
11. Two persons lifted up with a pole at the neck and dragged along floor.
12. Two persons pulled with left hand (right holding left wrist) on a pole.

13. A short loop over the neck and under the knees. Player tried to touch the rope above with feet.
14. Dart throw (one chance) with the left hand and with the right hand.
15. Hopping on the rump with both feet up in the air, held together.
16. Hopping on knuckles and stiff legs.
17. Distance hop on the left foot, then the right foot, and then back onto left foot.
18. Distance hop on left hand.
19. Rabbit hop for distance with legs between hands.
20. Pushing against sharp stick at upper lip.
21. High jump with the knee aimed at hitting a rope.
22. Pushing against an opponent with the head under the right shoulder.

The games were played both as individual and as team sports. Women also played with each other. In these Christmas games, the elderly Lois Cleveland, who had a large repertoire of Eskimo games, and her two daughters joined the event. There were, however, more men participating. It was the Iñupiaq cultural venue for the young to learn to sharpen their skills at these traditional forms of physical contest.

The gaming procedure was pleasantly informal and low-key, consistent with the Iñupiaq behavior style. Each team member sat at opposite sides of the room. A team captain would announce a competition. Contestants sat patiently until one person got up, for example, to pick up a rope or the four-foot-long pole and take up his position at the center of the floor. Then a contestant from the other side would step up. If the contestants did not have the position right, others would shout out instructions to correct it. Elders, including Lois Cleveland, were the game authorities and advisors and often started the game to show how it was played. Once a contestant won, another from the opposite side stepped up to challenge. The winning side was declared when no one from the opposing team stepped out to meet the challenge. The point was marked for that side to be tallied up at the end of the games for that night.

By 1979, the Selawik Christmas celebration at the Friends Church had grown more elaborate. A mimeographed "Noel Program" announced 117 presentations and performances by adults and children (see appendix 3). The Selawik spirit of Christmas continued to bring about the sharing of happy times and good cheer. The celebration was one of community spirit, a sense of being together as fellow Siilaviŋmiut.

SNO-GO CULTURE

The introduction of the snowmobile vastly benefited and transformed Iñupiaq hunting practices. Hunters could travel much farther in search of small clusters of animals that roam the region. With the speed of the snowmobile, they usually traveled and returned to the village on the same day. By the 1970s, hunting by dog team, which in the past had been carried out in small groups—or at least a pair of men who ventured out for weeks at a time—was quite rare.

Snowmobiles impacted winter travel in other ways, some unanticipated and others more precarious. Travel time between villages or on hunting forays was so much reduced that impulsive youths frequently started out on a trip underprepared. But snowstorms could suddenly arise or a snowmobile could break down and the traveler would be caught without proper clothing or camping gear. In the past, when traveling by dog team, the dogs would always be able to find their way back home for their master. By 1970, such unanticipated events had become so dangerously frequent that safety measures were implemented. Selawik was among the first villages in the region to organize a search and rescue organization, in 1970, to service the community in the summers as well as winters. The Selawik Search and Rescue had a president, volunteer members, and an operating fund, originally raised from village bingo nights and carnival events.

Each year, members of the organization snowmobiled out to stake a trail by erecting wooden guideposts with a crossbar, set at intervals between villages to help guide winter travelers on the snowy path and alleviate the likelihood of getting lost en route. One oral account told of a young Noorvik man leaving his village on a clear day to visit his Selawik girlfriend but running into a snowstorm on the way. He got lost in the blizzard, and when his snowmobile dropped off a high point on the path, he was pinned down by the machine. He was lightly dressed. He was eventually found but lost an arm to frostbite. In the summer of 1977, when we were in the village, a young Selawik man in an outboard motorboat was out on the river and his boat was found floating with no one in it. The Selawik Search and Rescue boat team was dispatched from the village. An additional ten rescue team members from Kiana flew in, and more members from Noorvik and Ambler arrived to assist. They finally found the young man's body. The emergency operation attested to close cooperation between Selawik and Kobuk villagers.

During the long, dark days of winter, when most people were at home, not in the fish camps, the village service organizations were much in operation. As with Search and Rescue, organizations were set up formally, with officers nominated and voted on in a manner that harked back to the very first days of Selawik village life. These organizations included as the Dog Mushers, the Volunteer Fire Department, the City Council, and the City Advisory Board. The Mothers' Club had a visible role in village funerals as women pooled their stitching skills to make coffin linings and a new set of clothing for the deceased and prepared food for all the guests. Selawik people's long experience of forming local organizations made it not too formidable a task to later integrate other state and national organizations like the National Guard and Head Start into their daily lives. Historically, the entire governmental organization of the city—introduced by John Collier back in the days of Roosevelt's New Deal—was readily adopted by the village. This included the incorporation of the village in 1939, three years after the federal Alaska Reorganization Act that created the positions of the mayor and postmaster as well as a clinic with a nurse aide staff.

THE COMING OF SPRING

The arrival of songbirds around the beginning of April announced the approach of spring or *upingaksrak*, meaning just about summer. One began to sense some warmth in the sun's rays, and the days became noticeably longer.

Another announcement of spring was break-up of the Selawik River. Traces of melted water began to appear around the edges of the river and lakes. It was still possible to cross the river in Selawik in late May, although one had to carefully wade through slippery melted ice along the shore to get to the dry areas in the middle of the river. It was intimidating to slosh through six inches of melted ice without knowing whether the river was still hard underneath. Again, as during the freeze-up, one looked for the warning willow branches.

Snowmobile racing in May, within the village and between villages, brought in an exciting spring intermission. The major race was the annual long-distance sno-go race from Kotzebue to Selawik to Kiana and Noorvik and back to Kotzebue. With an air of celebration, spectators lined the waypoints in each village to cheer the racers. Most contestants entered this long-distance race for the challenge of the long, hard race, additionally spurred on by big reward money. The trail between villages, littered with broken snowmobile parts, attested to the hard driving the contestants had put into their race. One Euro-American contestant who entered just for the experience of it stopped to rest in villages along the route. When all the other racers had come in at the finish in Kotzebue and his arrival was too long overdue, Kotzebue Search and Rescue dispatched their rescue team out—only to find him comfortably sleeping and resting in a village.

By the long daylight days of June, the snow melts rapidly, and by mid-June only patches of winter drift snow remain. And, to greet the oncoming summer days, were the mosquitos.

8

Long Days and the Summer Rhythm

Summer life in Selawik had its own rhythm, marked by the gradual warming and longer hours of sunlight. A unique sight in the middle of the summer evening was the pale sun hanging low on the horizon and the rising moon at the other end of the sky. To a newcomer, this first sight evoked a sense of awe mixed with doubt as to whether it was a mirage.

People happily talked about "long days" arriving. With long daylight hours and no sunset, they woke up to new senses of life. Men thought about the prospect of hunting moose, caribou, and wild ducks on their migration routes. Women visualized fish—many, many of them that they could harvest from the Selawik River and lakes.

Wanni's fieldnotes of Wednesday, June 22, 1977, are illustrative:

> Visited Nellie Russell and had an excellent three-hour conversation with her. I was going to ask Nellie to keep a record of her fish catch, but then I found out that she had already taken her nets out from the Putlunnaaq slough and the Angaagoqaq slough at her family allotment.
>
> However, at my request, Nellie consented to allow me to count all the fish she had drying out on her racks and in strings. She even went out to help me count. Her two nets were put in around June 2, and yesterday, June 21, was the day the nets were taken out. For these 19 days of spring and early summer gill netting at her family allotment, the Russell family had, as of yesterday, 877 fish altogether. The greatest

https://doi.org/10.5876/9781646426065.c008

number is whitefish (589 fish), followed by pike (262 fish), shee (13 fish), and mud shark (11 fish). Sixty of them were frozen as dog feed. The figure, of course, did not include those that this family of seven members had consumed during the past two weeks and a half, those given to friends, those fed each day to the dogs, and those thrown away at the netting site because they were too spoiled to be of any use. Nellie mentioned that she used to get many more fish at her old netting site at Staayatkuchiak.

The fieldnote entry of Thursday, June 16, 1977, presents a comparative picture of another woman's fishing activity, which was more restricted at her fishing site:

Lona Wood rowed over to our place to give us a gift of fresh whitefish and a piece of shee fish which she knew we liked. We had fresh fish tonight for dinner.

Lona had only one net out in the river. She had no outboard motor boat, just a rowboat, and therefore had no transportation efficient enough for setting her net away from the village. She had only one son with her during the summer. The other son was away for the summer job at Hog River. They also had only 2 dogs to feed. Yesterday Lona got 8 pikes and today she got 5 whitefish and some pikes. Of the five whitefish she had obtained today, she gave one to us, two to her sister Nora, and two small ones to the dogs.

The two comparative fishing activities of the two women demonstrate the significance of multiple factors that contributed toward a rich fish harvest or a modest day-today harvest of fisherwomen. The Selawik Drainage System was known as being bountiful in its fish resources. It is most famous for its huge, delicious sheefish (sii).

Ecologically, Selawik River does not have the proper spawning grounds for salmon so it never experiences the salmon runs so important to Kobuk people. But Selawik River is known as the home of five kinds of whitefish (*qalupiaq*): the *qaaligiq* with its sharp pointed head; the *qausrilluk* with big, round nose; the *quptik* with small, sharp nose; the *qalusraaq*, the smallest whitefish; and particular to the Selawik Fish River, the whitefish named *ikkuiyiq*. All of these varieties inhabit the entire river system in great profusion and were netted throughout the year. Pike (*siulik*), as big as forty inches long, was likewise enjoyed. Fewer in number were the burbot, locally called mud shark (*tittaaliq*) by villagers; grayling (*sulukpauġaq*), which could be hooked in clear, running streams; and sucker (*milugiaq*). The small blackfish called *iluuqiniq* was known for its interesting survival skill: it hibernated in the muddy lake in winter and came back to life in spring. An anecdote tells of a man who got a frozen blackfish in spring. He put it in a pot of water to cook, and in a few minutes, it started to swim.

Summertime was when women were at their busiest. Each family put in two to four fish nets as soon as possible after break-up. All summer long the women put in long days harvesting fish, cutting and drying each day's catch to prevent spoiling. The only exception was on Sunday, church day, when all subsistence activities ceased, a practice introduced by the first Quaker missionaries. For families with fish camps farther away from the village, the time spent at the fish camp with their family was considered half-work, half-vacation time, where they could live in tents in the quiet and pristine wilderness.

Once dried, the whitefish and the pike would be strung together, eight fish to a string, to be saved for the winter food supply. A skilled fisherwoman with a rich harvest proudly counted her total catch in bundles. A bundle of fish had an accumulation of twenty-five fish strings. In 1977, one family with three daughters to help had put in two nets, from spring until June 23. They returned from their fish camp with three bundles of whitefish and two bundles of pike, that is, 600 whitefish and 300 pike. Their total season harvest of 900 fish was considered one of the best in the village. Sheefish, due to their big size, were each kept separately, unstrung. Fish cutting and drying activities declined sharply when the summer temperature went above 75 degrees Fahrenheit, both because of the discomfort of working in such a warm temperature and because the fish tend to spoil in the heat if not processed the day of the catch. Rainy weather, which hampered the daily checking of the fish net, likewise contributed to poor fish harvest.

In late summer, even though classes at the village school had resumed by the first week of September, many mothers who needed extra hands in fish processing would let their daughters miss classes. The principal of the Selawik School had to be flexible and accommodating to the villagers' important subsistence demand and not penalize students for their absence. Other families, not wanting their children to miss school and fortunate enough to have their netting sites near the village, resorted to boating out daily to check their nets in the late afternoon and then staying up late in the evening to cut and hang the fish on the drying racks. Daughters were enculturated early to the art of fish cutting. They learned that the fish's head and backbone, to be saved as dog feed, had to be carefully severed as a separate piece from the edible meat piece.

By late fall, hardworking fisherwomen could be proud of their harvest. Women took great pride in their skill as fisherwomen who could provide their family with food security for the winter to come. Clara Ballot's fish count for summer 1977 exemplifies the fishing activity of a family with a dog team. Her family had nine dogs and five puppies. Clara worked hard. From her two fish nets, she got approximately 2,493 whitefish, 737 pike, 61 sheefish, and 33 mud shark—not counting the fish she gave away to friends. Lenora Skin's count of two months (September and

Figure 8.1. Marie Clark and her fish-drying rack, 1968.

October) from her two fish nets listed 1,006 whitefish, 171 pike, 5 sheefish, and 7 mud shark. According to Lenora, September had yielded a poor harvest because "it was too wet." Appendix 2 provides a more detailed picture of the two women's fishing activities.

Fishing season was over around the end of October. A number of women who were not constrained by the schooling of children stayed at their fish camps until the very end of the season.

The Selawik area has its own distinctive habitat. A Kobuk woman marrying in, coming to live in Selawik, and wishing to become a competent Selawik fisher-woman needed to learn more about this different environment and different fish behavior. Fish functioned as the main subsistence diet of the riverine Iñupiat. As a home-cooked meal, fish were boiled or steam-boiled. Steam-boiled half-dried fish—that is, a fish that was dried only for a few days—was considered a delicacy. In the winter, cut-up frozen fish morsels called *quaq* resembled Japanese sashimi. On any trip in which the traveler desired a light load, or on a berry-picking foray toward the end of the summer, dried fish served well as a travel food. *Tinuksuvak* was a dish of dried, crushed fish eggs and fish liver mixed with oil and wild cranberries. In a sweeter version, sugar replaced the oil. It was considered a special traditional dish to compete with *akutaq*, which consisted of creamed fat, meats, and berries, humorously referred to by non-Iñupiaq outsiders as Eskimo ice cream,

The role of fish in traditional Iñupiat lifeways was made more evident when, in spring 1977, the Alaska Department of Fish and Game limited the caribou take to only two caribou per family. The regulation forced women to increase their fishing activities that summer in order to ensure a sufficient supply of food for the winter. Even young women previously not interested or involved in fishing got into the act. A twenty-nine-year-old woman was observed learning for the first time from her prospective mother-in-law how to cut fish for drying. The head of that family was the custodian of the village school and was definitely not short of funds for buying white man's food. But traditional food was important, and her family did not want to be deprived of it. Fish and Game sent in free beef roasts to help alleviate the meat shortage. Yet, as one Selawiker commented, the beef "didn't taste good."

At fish camp, while women were busy with fish netting, the men pursued their favorite activity—hunting. Occasionally, a moose or a caribou would wander into the area, a sought-after game to be hunted to satisfy their hunger for fresh meat. What was left over was shared with their extended family and friends back in the village, who were just as hungry for fresh meat. Migrating wild ducks, ptarmigans, hares, and muskrats were all hunted. Selawik was known as a rich area for muskrats, whose skins were used for making the warm and beautifully designed winter parka. Kobuk Iñupiat used to acquire their muskrat skins from Selawik, but by the 1970s, due to the accessibility of modern store-bought synthetic parka, which were lighter and easier care for, the demand for muskrat skins had fallen off.

The summer subsistence cycle closed with the wild-berry-picking season. Women eagerly waited for the berries they had been watching over to be ready for harvesting. They had been eyeing locations where a particular kind of berry bushes was spotted. They were especially concerned about the winds, which could blow away the salmonberry blossoms and damage the hoped-for harvest. Salmonberries (*aqpik*), the first berries to ripen, and lowbush cranberries (*kikminnaq*) were the berries most picked. Both grew easily. Because salmonberries were particularly sensitive to wind damage, the cranberry harvest was usually more abundant. Following the peak of salmonberry season, blueberries (*asriavik*) began to ripen, easily harvested by a wooden scoop (*qalutok*). Wild strawberries (*ivrum asriq*, meaning grass berries) were sweet red surprises that could be found in tall grass. Blackberries (*paungaq*) were also harvested, though to a much lesser extent.

Often, the whole family joined in harvesting wild berries and greens, an enjoyable all-day outing that got them away from busy village life. They picnicked together. Many women with jobs outside the village made a special trip home during this period, just for the pleasure of berry-picking with the family. Ruthie Sampson, who used to go berry-picking with her mother but was working in Rhode Island with Wanni on a book during one harvest season, commiserated, "I really miss berry-picking." Wanni's fieldnotes of Wednesday, July 27, 1977, narrated similar sentiment in another family:

> On the walk back home from the airport, I could not resist picking the grass berries which were in abundance among the grass on the trail between the Ticket's burned house and our place. Got a small sandwich bag full.
>
> A lot of women went berry-picking now. The women loved berry-picking. Yesterday Rhoda Skin said that as soon as she got home from Kotzebue (where she worked as a waitress in a restaurant), her mother said, "Let's go berry-picking." Her parents, Arthur and Lenora, Rhoda, her brother Chubby, and her niece Betty, left this afternoon in their boat up the Niġraq Channel for berry-picking. Some of the blueberries were already ripe. The blueberries here ripened later than those on the Kobuk. Salmonberries were ready. Some were already too ripe.
>
> Of the wild berries grown around the Selawik terrain, salmonberries were the most plentiful.

Harvested berries ware kept in storage barrels. A used Blazo can came in handy as a storage container. Women with freezers stored berries in plastic bags. Storage methods had changed since the past, when they were kept in skin pokes in the underground storage, and women now took advantage of the new Western materials and technology. An elderly woman was quite happy that for the coming 1977 winter she managed to get five barrels of cranberries and one barrel of blueberries. She wished she had gotten more salmonberries.

Edible tubers sought in the wild were the Eskimo potato (*masru*) and the plant called *pitniq*, which has a white edible part under its brown skin. It was boiled like *masru*. Another wild plant that no woman would pass up if she spotted it was wild rhubarb (*qusrimmaq*). Rhubarb dessert, Selawik-style according to May Walton, was to cut both the stems and the leaves and boil them together. Tasters could later add as much sugar as they wanted. According to Nellie Russell, if they caught a pike full of roe, its roe was mashed and whipped, then mixed with mashed cranberries into an Iñupiaq delicacy called *ittukpaluk* (Lee, Sampson, and Tennant 1992:207). Sourdock, Eskimo celery (*ikuusuq*), and wild rose hips were likewise enjoyed. When seal oil obtained from the coast turned rancid, adding wild vegetables like Eskimo celery helped to improve its taste. The tip of spring willows (*saura*) could be eaten soaked in seal oil, with vinegar and sugar added for better flavor.

The American celebration of the Fourth of July gave Selawikers an occasion to celebrate. Each Iñupiaq village planned the celebration differently. The essential goal was to have fun together while incorporating Iñupiaq cultural elements into the national icon to make the day the Iñupiaq Fourth of July. In Selawik, members of the Selawik Dog Mushers Association organized the day's events. The celebration was held at the airport with its wide, open space, and it would be teeming with children. They competed in a variety of competitions for different age groups, including foot races, a bicycle race, and a gunnysack-hopping contest. Men competed at rifle shooting, and young men and women competed in an egg-throwing contest. In some villages, a Miss Fourth of July beauty contest was not only a venue to showcase pretty young Iñupiaq girls and the beautifully sewn parkas that they wore but also an occasion to emphasize the significance of Iñupiaq culture, specifically women's traditional sewing skills. In Selawik in 1977, the Fourth of July beauties were babies, gurgling and cutely clothed in skin maklaks and baby outfits. They were judged by both their traditional Iñupiaq outfits and their interaction style. The winner was a little girl who smiled happily at everyone.

For men, summer was the time to earn extra money. During the salmon run in the latter part of the summer, a few families who owned bigger boats for ocean fishing and were willing to buy the expensive commercial fishing license from the state's Fish and Game office would go to Kotzebue to join others from the Noatak and Kobuk villages. They would sell their catch to the salmon commercial fishing cooperative that was set up in Kotzebue. Women who went along could bring in extra cash income if they got hired as fish cutters.

Toward the end of the summer when the oil barge arrived with the winter oil and gas supply as well as school supplies for the coming academic year, a number of strong young men got temporary longshoring jobs. A few lucky men with carpenter skills might get short-term building contracts in Kotzebue or elsewhere. The jobs brought in a good cash income, but the men had to live apart from their families. Like on the Kobuk (D. Anderson et al. 1998), occasional cash-income employment enabled Selawikers to be more efficient in their traditional subsistence practices. They could use the money to purchase their boat's outboard motor, snowmobiles, and other items that their other sources of income could not cover.

As the heat of the summer grew more intense—as high as 100 degrees Fahrenheit—and the wild grass became drier, many locations throughout Alaska faced the danger of forest or tundra fires. Selawik villagers were on the watch. By the end of the first week of July 1977, five tundra fires had already been spotted around Selawik. Men were frequently seen standing on the riverbank with their binoculars trained on the horizon, trying to spot a telltale smoky trail. They were anxious to ensure that the forest fire was under control and their natural subsistence habitat not ruined. Alaska's forest-fire management brought in another form of income earning for able-bodied adults.

Wanni's fieldnotes of July 24, 1977, recorded the news on the CB radio transmission announcing that as many as 1,200 forest fires were burning throughout

Alaska. The State of Alaska Division of Forestry and the US Bureau of Land Management worked together to put out the fires. Firefighting crews from different villages were called in, then airlifted out to the burning sites. When the call came in to a village, the village crew boss would send out a message on CB radio and by word of mouth to notify anyone interested to join the crews. A supplementary crew that year, called the "emergency crew," was organized as a standby. Douglas wanted to learn about this activity, so he signed up for the last crew but was disappointed that it was not called out. A volunteer had to be between eighteen and sixty years of age to be eligible. Each crew, consisting of sixteen men and women, could bring along a woman as cook. The group's preparation to go out as firefighters was an exciting event in the village, as young men and women hurriedly packed for the departure. They loaded their backpacks with an extra pair of trousers with narrow legs, a good pair of rubber boots that would not melt in the heat, and, when going to tundra terrain, an extra pair of socks, a good pair of gloves, and soap. The Bureau of Land Management would supply firefighters with an emergency kit of sleeping bag, mosquito net, mosquito repellent, and other equipment. The income that could be earned on this job, paid by the hour, was quite substantial. For the sociable Iñupiat, the job brought along team camaraderie, an opportunity to show individual competence, and another byproduct, the opportunity to see a new place and meet people from other villages. It was also an occasion for young men to practice speaking Iñupiat with their older relatives, something they were usually too shy to try in their own village. Selawik firefighting crews were well respected. It was a source of pride in Selawik that their crews were the first to be called in each summer. The only negative aspect of the job was the celebration after their wages were paid. A number of young men had a tendency to work hard and play hard. Sometimes they celebrated too hard, wasting their hard-earned money on liquor and getting drunk, to the disappointment and anger of their family.

For school-age children, Culture Camp was an opportunity to venture outside the village at the end of July. It was organized by a regional Iñupiaq nonprofit foundation, the Aqqaluk Trust, founded by Robert Aqqaluk Newlin Sr. of Noorvik, who wanted young Iñupiat to master traditional culture while learning other subjects at the government's public schools. Camp attendance was voluntary. Children were divided into four ages groups: 7–9 years, 9–11, 11–14, and 14 years to collage age. The campground was at Camp Sivunniivik, near Noorvik, on the Kobuk River. For one fun week, the children were taught traditional Iñupiaq subsistence skills, from trapping, fishing, and fish-cutting to berry-picking. The children returned home to Selawik happy from camping and having met and befriended children from other villages on the Kobuk.

AN INDIAN SCARE

A hapless incident unsettled the summer rhythm of 1994. Wanni's July 24 fieldnotes recorded it:

> Saw William and Esther Sheldon. Esther was quite worried about her son, Collins, who was working with Doug on the dig upriver. Collins was supposed to come back into the village this evening. She commented that she hoped he did not have to come into town alone. She said that a pilot spotted a group of wild men walking somewhere upriver between the Selawik River and the Kobuk River. According to Esther, when the wild men saw the plane, one of them went to hide among the trees. It sounded like another dangerous stranger /Indian scare. I tried to console Esther not to be too worried because Collins would be coming in on a speed boat, not walking on land. She inquired what time Collins would be coming back. I gave her sometime between 8.30–9 PM, the time he had come back the previous Sunday. I didn't know if that was any consolation. When I walked back home, William was standing at the high point on the bridge which gave a panoramic view a long way, looking upriver. So William was also worried. He told me that if Collins did not come back tonight, we should go upriver tomorrow to check on him and the expedition group to make sure they were all right.

As it turned out, it was not the pilot but a passenger on her flight home from Kotzebue to Noorvik village on the Kobuk River who spotted the suspicious group. The alarming news spread like wildfire from Noorvik to Selawik. Many Iñupiaq legends told about the past Iñupiaq-Athapaskan ethnic conflicts and ugly raids. A Selawik boy who visited us at the isolated, far end of the village across from the graveyard even impishly tried to spook us one day with a possible encounter with a scary *irrusriq* (spirit). Given the local legend about the unknown, the ominous entity, and the Iñupiaq moral code of responsibility for the safety of everyone in their area, their anxiety was not to be taken lightly. The mystery of the wild men was not solved until three days later, when a Selawik Wild Life Refuge worker in Kotzebue clarified Wanni's inquiry that a vegetation study group from the University of Arizona was around there to conduct research. It became a case of failed communication. Outsiders were rarely briefed about the Iñupiaq code of conduct prior to venturing into the area. Nevertheless, it was not irrational for villagers to expect to be informed about incoming persons or group as strictly practiced by the locals.

Collins safely arrived back at the village, his family's relief.

VILLAGE DIVERSITY

Selawik as a village grew in many ways during the twenty-six-year span of our visits. The population increased from 447 persons (eighty households) in 1969 to over

600 persons by 1994. Children we had met in the late 1960s became mature young adults. Some were married with children, and a few had moved away for jobs, especially to Anchorage and Kotzebue. Tragically, a number of them had passed away from accidental death or suicide.

When we first arrived in 1968, we noticed the prevalence of population diversity in Selawik similar to what we saw in Kiana village on the Kobuk River. Although the majority of families traced their ancestry back to much earlier times in Northwest Alaska, a few families had ancestors from the outside. Some showed phenotypic traits of other populations. One Euro-American man had long lived in the village with his Selawik wife and two daughters. An elderly woman lived with a biracial grandson, the son of her daughter married to a Euro-American man. Another of her daughters married a Euro-American serviceman stationed in Germany. A grocery store owner was half Selawik Iñupiaq and half Koyukon Athapaskan; he presented a strong affiliation with his Iñupiaq identity, contributing 25 percent of his income to the Friends Church. Interracial and interethnic marriages were socially perpetuated into the next generation. To Iñupiat who loved children, the comment "they have cute children" reflected the sentiment and acceptance of such unions. Our next-door neighbor welcomed a Native American daughter-in-law whom their son had met while attending the Bureau of Indian Affairs' Native boarding school in Chemawa, Oregon. In 1994 we met an African American postmaster in the village, married to a Selawik woman. A high school graduate married an Egyptian man, whom the family held in high regards for his strong support of his wife's college education after marriage. Three Euro-American Selawik School teachers met, married, and settled in Selawik with their Selawik Iñupiaq wives. We attended the wedding of a woman Selawik schoolteacher to an Iñupiaq young man from the Kobuk River, a crew member on Douglas's archaeological excavation at Onion Portage. In all the time we spent in Selawik, we never once encountered any tension between individuals based on their ancestral origins. In fact, the long-standing diversity of the village population and the regularity of compromises across groups contributed quite positively to Selawik's less-confrontational politics, in contrast to what is often seen in small villages.

Summertime as a whole was a pleasant time for the older generation. The weather was kinder to their older bodies. With no slippery ice, they could move around more easily. Oftentimes, the elders would sit in front of their homes to enjoy the quiet peace of the evening hours, catch the cool breeze, enjoy the colorful sunset, and socialize with people who walked by. With the long days of summer and no school, children stayed out late into the night to play on the walking paths or beside the riverbank until it was too dark to see. The curfew bell from the Friends Church tolled at eleven p.m. to remind them that it was time to go home to bed.

9

The Selawik Wolves and the Maklak Telegraph

In the Iñupiaq historical past, the *kargi* was the social center of the community. It was the place where men came together to learn how to make subsistence tools, had lunch, and told stories to one other. It was the place the community convened for gatherings, held dances and feasts, and entertained visitors from other communities (W. Anderson 2005).

The present-day two-room Selawik Community Hall, sitting in the center of the village on Akuliġaq Island, held similar social and political functions. At the end of the twentieth century, these activities had expanded to meet present-day needs and happenings. It was still the focal place of reference, where the village city council held their meetings, where incoming guests gave talks, and, in the summer, where village firefighting crews and crew bosses met to organize. It was the only public social space large enough to accommodate the serving of meals to funeral guests. A small storage room to one side of the wooden building was often used as the village jail, mostly to let inebriated men cool off after a night of binge drinking. Homicide and other severe crimes rarely occurred in Selawik, and if they did, they were handled by state police brought in from the outside.

During the long, dark winter, the Community Hall was the social lifeline, especially for older women who gathered there after dinner to play bingo. The game provided a time away from home, social interactions with other players, and the risk-taking excitement of playing with money in the pot as an additional incentive. In the winter of 1971–1972, the game took place almost every night except on

https://doi.org/10.5876/9781646426065.c009

Sunday. It was organized by the Search and Rescue Committee, with the proceeds used to fund the village's emergency search and rescue operations, from marking winter trails to locating people lost on snowmobile trails in winter blizzards or drowned in summer boating accidents.

Before the introduction of television, the older generation derived a great deal of pleasure from tuning in to the "Eskimo Story" hour of the Kotzebue Radio Station, usually referred to as the KOTZ Station, which broadcast Iñupiaq folktales taped from storytellers in the region. Any good storyteller who happened to be in Kotzebue on a hospital visit or visiting with relatives could drop by the station to tell their stories. The day after a broadcast, people would be talking about this or that person telling the stories they had heard the night before. The story would then be passed on to those who had missed the program. Good storytellers derived a great deal of pride from their broadcast and received heartwarming compliments from fellow villagers. During the 1960s, the host of this popular program was a capable Selawik young woman named Helen Davis.

Old Iñupiaq stories were also passed between villages through recorded tapes that friends and relatives sent back and forth as unsolicited gifts or as Christmas presents, complete with family messages, greetings and best wishes, a recorded song, or a story or two to entertain. During the period in which tape recordings were popular, the new technology served effectively as the purveyor of goodwill, cemented long-distance social relationships, and assisted in the transmission of the Iñupiaq culture of storytelling and singing.

For families with a CB radio transmitter, Selawik mornings started with a bright, cheerful "Good morning" from the radio operator who happened to be the first to wake up. Invariably, the greeting was reciprocated with other CB radio transmitters joining in this spread of good cheers for the new day. CB transmissions had long held a positive vibe in the region. The "Maklak Telegraph," as it was fondly dubbed, served a vital role as a means of quick long-distance communication between villages before the introduction of the telephone. Families who could afford the cost invested in a CB radio.

There was neither an airport hangar nor an airport office in Selawik. Pilots on inbound flights into the village had long relied on "Selawik 1," the CB radio operated by Emma Norton (figure 9.1), a cousin of the Selawik-born Kotzebue charter flight pilot Don Ferguson, to inform them about the wind direction for safe landing.

In 1977, nine CB transmitters were in operation. By 1994, with easier access to purchase and lower prices, there were 120 citizens communicating on CB. Its role as a viable channel of communication both within the village and across villages grew. Within the village, greetings and news were passed, village meetings called, illness and health emergency communicated to the village nurse's aide, and many business

Figure 9.1. Emma Norton (left) and Wanni Anderson, 1971.

transactions conducted via the CB. A person on a boat trip with a CB radio could communicate their whereabouts back to their family. Should they run into problem, they could relay back to the village for help. News of an elderly person facing the last few days of life and of persons who had just passed away were relayed by CB so that relatives and friends from other villages could be informed and arrange the trip to the funeral.

With no movie theater, no restaurant, no coffee shop, and no shopping mall, social life for the young generation was confined to visiting with each other, boating around during the summer, and snowmobiling during the winter. One sports activity that took a strong hold on the young men was basketball. The basketball hoop in front of the school building was always busy after school hours with young boys practicing shooting baskets. When the high school was established and a large gym constructed, Selawik basketball players had a regular basketball court on which to practice. They hit the court with a bang and became the symbol and the pride of the village. In inter-village competition, the Selawik Wolves managed to beat other teams in the Arctic Northwest region and in 1994 earned the title of NANA Regional Champions. Loyal supporters flew or sno-go-ed to nearby villages on the

Figure 9.2. Selawik Wolves logo.

Kobuk to cheer their home team. Selawik High School cheerleaders could be seen in white cheerleading outfits. Rotman's, the main village grocery store, proudly displayed a shelf of Selawik Wolves sweatshirts and T-shirts (figure 9.2).

Selawik children loved to ice skate, and they could buy skates at Rotman's. As soon as the river began to freeze along the edge, the children were out skating back and forth over the narrow patch. When the river was completely frozen but before snow covered the ice, a group of children would skate to the frozen Niglaktuk Lake close to the village. Our house, the only one on the Nigraq Creek, was a happy rest stop for skaters (figure 9.3). They arrived to warm themselves for a while, see inside "the Cupcake House," as the children dubbed our house, then went back to the lake to resume their skating fun before returning again to warm up. The skaters plied us with endless questions and delighted us with their stories. But speed skating, which could very well have developed into a strong village sport for the young waited, was yet to be introduced.

James Ede, the principal of the Selawik School who had extensive Alaska school contacts, happened to acquire secondhand skates that had been left behind in school lockers in Fairbanks. He sent for them and put them on sale at the school

Figure 9.3. Children skating in front of Nigraq Channel, 1971.

economically at $1.30–$3.00 a pair, just to cover the cost of shipment. Schoolchildren were happy to acquire them since they were cheaper than at Rotman's. As the skating group grew in number, an innovative game was born. Wanni's fieldnotes of November 19, 1971, narrated:

> The river on the other side of our house at the tip of the island is today free of snow because of the wind. After our dinner, around 6.30 PM, we heard voices of children talking, laughing, and yelling not too far away. I went out to investigate and found a large group of them skating. I stood watching them and talked to those who took a break from skating for about an hour. During that hour, more and more children came to join the play group that by the time I left, included about 17 children from 6 to 13 years old. The Skins' children were also there with flashlights which they used to light their way from their home. They did not turn off their flashlights during the skating. The river skating area had no light. The closest source of light was a small village light, about 150 feet away. One could see only dark forms moving, the swishing sound of the skates on the ice, and the sound of the children once in a while calling and stopping to talk to each other. The flashlights made moving light spots like fireflies in the dark. I watched them for a while before I realized that they were playing Tag on skates. The kid who was "It" tried to hide the fact that he was, facilitated by the darkness. It added to the surprise and the excitement of the game, for the players

had no way of knowing if another player approaching him was "It" or not. They played the game until the curfew hour of 9.00 PM.

A birthday party, an occasion for happy reunion, broke the monotony of the village routine. All day long, the CB transmissions would buzz with "Happy Birthday" wishes to the birthday person. A birthday was celebrated with a dinner feast among family members and close friends. It was not incongruent to see the Iñupiaq caribou stew served with macaroni and cheese, dried fish, seal oil, and Eskimo ice cream sitting side-by-side with bread, Jell-O, canned fruits, a variety of pies, and a nice birthday cake.

For some families, group dinners among friends and family members who lived in different households were frequent social events. "Food eaten together tastes more delicious," pronounced Nora Norton, whose home was the setting of many friendly dinners.

A young Selawiker experimented with bringing in movies to show for a small charge in the Community Hall. Selawik School principal Jim Ede showed free movies in the school gym. Westerns held great appeal, as the kids excitedly cheered the buffalo-hunting scene or when the hero beat the villains or the "bad Indians." The natural setting of the arid Southwest, so different from their frigid Arctic environment, magnified the attraction. So, too, were the films like *Tuktu and the Kayak* and *The Eskimo Family*, produced in Canada, that depicted Canadian Inuit life, which they found fascinating. Ede ordered many documentaries to familiarize Selawikers with the outside world. Horror movies were also kids' favorite. They squealed. They screeched. They screamed, then laughed at their own silly fright.

Later on, when television came in, many people was hooked. In some homes the television was turned on all the time as men resumed their interest in Westerns and expanded their scope to include national news and nature shows. Older women with time on their hands indulged in soap dramas. The home environment could turn quite noisy, hard for conversation, with the television and the CB transmission both blaring. Young people were not as tuned in to the television programs as the older generation since they preferred a more active life in the public spaces rather than being confined inside the house. When they stayed in, some congregated in the makeshift pool hall, a one-room old house on the island that was formerly the village *kargi*. It was in a way a perpetuation of the former traditional men's house.

SPRING CARNIVAL: THE SELAWIK VENUE

In 1972, Noorvik, the village on the Kobuk closest to Selawik, organized a spring carnival during the first week of April. The carnival served as an important social milieu for the Kobuk-Selawik connectedness. The April temperatures, still below freezing, enabled Selawikers to travel to Noorvik quite easily on snowmobiles, taking along family members or friends. A sled would be hitched on to carry luggage and to provide a more comfortable ride for bigger or older women. Only the young rode the snowmobile straddling the driver. Those with more travel funds flew over. The Selawik-Noorvik snowmobile trail marked the safest and shortest route for riders to follow. A snowmobile trip, if running smoothly, took only two to three hours. Iñupiat fondly nicknamed this modern, useful vehicle "sno-go." At the carnival, they enjoyed the fun of the competitive races and visiting with friends and relatives living on the bank of another river.

During the last week of April, Selawikers organized their own spring carnival. The school and the village organizations joined hands for the festivities. In addition to guests flying over and arriving by snowmobiles, they delightedly welcomed Noorvik dog team racers arriving with their families and their dogs. They were happy to see a Euro-American dog team racer and schoolteacher Pete MacManus coming all the way from Ambler.

The Selawik School hosted the first day's event in the school building. While the Mothers' Club and the Student Council staffed the snack bar, the village Medical Fund was in charge of the bingo game, which would replenish their useful health fund. The Mothers' Club, with more women lending their hands, handled two other fun games, the fish pond and the cake walk. The City Council's game, the dime toss, went broke shortly after its opening. Those still challenged by the precision skill that they were good at tried their hands at the dart throw. Children had fun watching cartoons in a school classroom. Wanni's fieldnotes of the day described:

> Helped at the school to make a carnival jail for the carnival tonight. We used cardboard papers, painted on the jail bar motif with a cut-up window on one side. A player could put someone in jail for 10 cents. The prisoner could pay the fine of the same amount to get out or had to stay in jail for 15 minutes. . . . The jail setup didn't attract the adults. . . . The kids, on the other hand, were fascinated. Instead of letting someone else put them in jail, half of the kids paid themselves to be jailed. They jumped around, telling everyone who passed by excitedly, "I am in jail! I am in jail!" They even liked the idea of not getting out.
>
> The village earned $18 that day from the jail game. Three kids repeatedly bought tickets to get in and out of jail.

The Spook House, which derived its inspiration from the children's enjoyment of horror films, opened late that night because the setup took a long time to complete. It was quite popular among the kids. Some of them, even eighth graders, went through quite fast, not daring to look at the scary things set up inside. Screams emitted from those who dared to look.

Figure 9.4. William
Sheldon (son of Ikik),
former reindeer herder
and president of the
Selawik Dog Mushers
Association, 1972.

Over the following days, festivities included foot races, snowmobile races, and
dog team races organized by the Dog Mushers Association with William Sheldon
as president of the association that year (figure 9.4).

The frozen Selawik River turned into a racetrack. Snowmobile races were
divided into men's and women's categories and three different horsepower types,
starting with the light 14–18 HP Skidoo or Polaris. The second category was the
26–29 HP snowmobile, and the most powerful was the 30–34 HP category. The
racers paid a $10 entrance fee and had to race three rounds from the north end of
the village to the south end, the track marked by oil drums. Since snowmobiles
functioned as the current winter mode of transportation, young women were
skilled snowmobile riders. Amid the light snowfall that day, they enthusiastically
participated in the races.

Dog-team racing was spread out over three days because of the length of the race
course, the long race time involved, and the men's teams being given two chances at
the competition (figure 9.5).

Figure 9.5. A twelve-dog team race contestant comes in to the finish line, 1972.

Three women's teams, including one from Noorvik, competed in the eight-dog category. Their race course on the river ice covered eleven miles. Since the number of families raising race dogs had dwindled, one woman had to assemble her dog team from the dogs from two families. The other Selawik racer drove her older brother's dog team.

The longer-distance men's dog team race on the twenty mile-course generated the greatest excitement, even more than the snowmobile races. Eight teams, three from Selawik, four from Noorvik, and one from Ambler, competed in the race with nine to eleven dogs in the team. They competed again the next day. The top racer made it back to the village in less than two hours. The Coffins from Noorvik made history that year, winning first place in both the men's and women's races. As the teams raced in, people whistled, hooted, and hollered. They excitedly encouraged the teams on with "ya-hoo" and "haw" shouts and cheers (figure 9.6).

On the afternoon of the second day, a Wien Air plane brought in the Kotzebue Community High School Band to give a concert, conducted by a music teacher from Arizona who had just arrived to teach at the Kotzebue High School. This was a new form of music for Selawikers. The conductor familiarized his audience with each Western musical instrument before the performance. After the finale, the band received enthusiastic applause from the audience.

For two evenings, Selawik resident guitar player Elwood Goode and his rock band of a drummer and three guitar players, two from neighboring Noorvik, performed in the armory building beyond the school building. The band had performed locally in several villages in the region. The young crowd had a lot of fun and danced until two a.m.

Figure 9.6. Tillie Ticket, Donna Norton, and Beverly Davis at the Selawik spring carnival, 1972.

Selawik entertained about a hundred visitors during the carnival week that year. According to the record kept by Nora and Emma Norton, the largest group to arrive, with forty participants, came from the closest village, Noorvik. Sixteen arrived from Kiana, the next-closest village. Seven came from Ambler and six from Buckland. Besides the Kotzebue High School band members, three visitors came from Kotzebue and three from Kobuk.

On the last day of the dog team race, a walkie-talkie message was relayed from the race monitors that a big herd of caribou was crossing the race course upriver. The herd had to be chased out of the way so that the race would not be interrupted. That afternoon, the sight that incited a loud, excited "ooh" from the spectators was of a snowmobile racing in from the direction of racers. A caribou head was dramatically mounted on the bar handle, its body trailing into the backseat. The hunter riding proudly into the village was a Kotzebue man. He was traveling to Selawik to enjoy the races, but when he came across the migrating herd, he could not resist the hunt. When the race was over, other hunters eagerly hopped on their snowmobiles towing the sled, racing upriver. The first spring caribou hunt of the northward migration started.

Figure 9.7. Sewing kits made by Lenora Skin, using sections of cloth in imaginative design.

SELAWIK ART

Selawik had a number of skilled local artists and craftspeople whose works were not widely known beyond the area. Not only did women pride themselves on their artistic skills at skin work, such as making muskrat parkas, they had an artistic flair for items they used in their daily lives. An example was the work of seamstress Lenora Skin, who cleverly stitched together colorful pieces of fabric in the manner of patchwork quilting for her cloth sewing kits (*irnaviret*) (figure 9.7).

Another older generation of artist we met was Nellie Russell, the only coiled-basket maker in Selawik (figure 9.8). Nellie, who was born near Kiana and whose mother had passed away, learned her art from elder Kotzebue women when she was growing up there with her father. Topcock (*pillangnak*) was the wild saltwater grass needed to construct this type of basket. She had to wait until fall for the grass to be dry enough to be collected for the purpose. Nellie's basket-making style had multicolored woolen store-bought yarn woven in horizontally as her aesthetic motif. Birchbark basket making was, however, not a developed skill among Selawik women as it was with those living in the forested Kobuk River area with more birch trees in their habitat.

Nellie also made needle cases, modeled after the ancient form no longer in use. Intricate beadwork can be observed in the photograph (figure 9.9).

The work of the well-known grandmother Effie Ramoth (daughter of Oglu Ballot) belongs in the domain of children's toys. Her work exemplified the close

Figure 9.8. Nellie Russell and one of her coiled baskets with colored yarn for decoration.

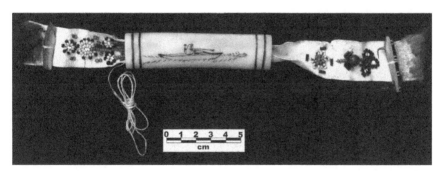

Figure 9.9. Needle case inspired by forms once used to protect bone needles, made by Nellie Russell.

bond between grandparents and grandchildren in Iñupiaq culture. One of her daughters, who was married and living elsewhere, sent her young son to live with Effie and keep her company. Effie made for her grandson a pair of Iñupiaq yo-yo of caribou skin with decorative fur trimming to play with. Under her instruction, her grandson excelled at it even as a young child. His expert demonstrations of the art of playing the yo-yo from the front, from the side, and above his head enticed other impressed customers to place more orders from his grandmother.

Other forms of art existed in the works of the next generation. May Walton is known as a skilled maker of caribou skin masks, inspired by the original mask style developed at Anaktuvuk Pass (figure 9.10). A carved wooden mold was first made, and then the wet caribou skin was stretched over it.

Leo Berry represents a younger generation of folk artist. As shown in figure 9.11, his mixed media art form consisted of caribou antler decorated with the masks of carved ivory, inspired by faces of old-time hunters/travelers wearing the traditional caribou-skin snow goggles and the chin tattoo.

Leslie Burnett, by contrast, was a commercial craftsman. He made souvenir toy sleds of wolverine jawbones and sinew for sale to tourists. His son-in-law, Delbert Mitchell, also an excellent artist, crafted exquisite miniature kayaks with caribou skin, finely stitched with caribou sinew (figure 9.12).

Norma Ballot, Iñupiaq teacher at the Selawik School, who trained in ivory carving while studying at the Kansas Art Institute, used a different medium. Her ivory jewelry was made from the walrus ivory she acquired from the immigration office's confiscated illegal ivory pieces. She considered her additional role as an Iñupiaq art teacher to be significant, and she trained a few interested young people in ivory and bone carving to instill this art form in the next generation.

SELAWIK HUMOR

The Iñupiat were brave, adventurous, resilient, hospitable, and sociable. They liked to laugh and joke and had a wonderful sense of humor. They never shied away from laughing at themselves. Many humorous anecdotes, passed on orally, told about the Iñupiat's first encounter with the white man and the white man's culture. The white man's food was disastrously strange to their taste. The white man was also a strange spectacle. A story tells about a little boy's first meeting with a white man:

> A little boy ran excitedly back home. He called loudly to his mother, "Aanaaŋ, Aanaaŋ, I just saw a very funny man. He was carrying a muskrat in his mouth!"
>
> The muskrat was a mouse-like animal whose skin was used for making the Iñupiaq traditional winter fur parka. The man the little boy saw was a white man with a dark, bushy beard!

Albert Wood, a frequent visitor to our house (figure 9.13), told a story of a man and his first mail order to the quintessential American retailer Sears and Roebuck:

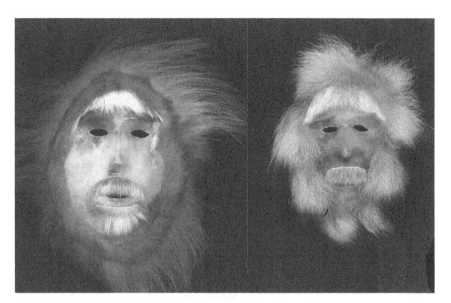

Figure 9.10. Caribou-skin masks made by May Walton.

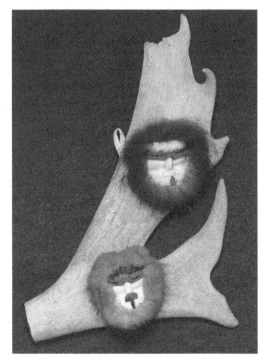

Figure 9.11. Plaque made by Leo Berry, son of Mabel and Frank Berry.

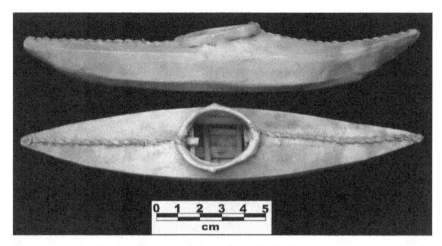

Figure 9.12. Caribou-skin kayak made by Delbert Mitchell.

When the white man's things first came into the village and mail-ordered Sears and Roebuck's catalogue first came in, an Eskimo man placed an order for an item in the catalogue. He waited eagerly for his order to come in.

Finally one day after a long wait, the postmaster told him that his order had arrived. The man was so happy. He rushed to the post office. There at the post office, he was given a box with a woman's dress in it.

"That's not what I ordered!" he wailed.

He was so disappointed. He thought he would be getting the beautiful young girl who wore that dress in the catalogue.

At the end of the story, Albert deftly delivered his punch line. "I wonder if he ordered a blonde or a brunette?"

Iñupiaq wit and sense of humor shine through in their repertoire of animal stories. Despite the fact that the Iñupiaq culture is a hunting culture, in their oral narratives they present wild animals with a great deal of humor. They are portrayed sometimes fondly, sometimes comically, oftentimes competing with or playing tricks on each other. The best-known tricksters in Iñupiaq oral literature are not men and women, as in many other storytelling cultures; they are the fox and the raven. "The Raven and the Fox," told by the premier Selawik storyteller, Nora Norton, in September 1968 (W. Anderson 2005:268–269) exemplifies how the two well-known tricksters were matched in wit. A woman unfortunately suffered the blunt of their joke:

There were two cross-cousins, Raven and Fox. This story tells about Raven and Fox who were making a living together.

Figure 9.13. Albert Wood with Wanni (in the shadow of the sled) on a trip to Kiana, 1972.

One time the two of them ran short of food, so Fox took off to the seashore to look for some food. Most likely he was looking for animal carcasses that might have drifted ashore.

Walking along the shore, Fox saw a small house, so he decided to check what sort of house that was. As he was standing at the door of the house, he heard someone coming to the door. Then he saw a large, fat woman who didn't appear to have a hard time as he did.

The woman came out of the house. When she saw Fox standing at the door, right away she asked, "How do I look? Am I a beautiful woman?"

Fox answered, praising the woman, "Oh yes, you are beautiful."

The woman invited Fox inside her house. She came back inside the house with dried fish in fish oil and berries. The woman wasn't beautiful at all, but the cunning Fox told her what she wanted to hear. He gave her a good answer, and he had a scrumptious meal. He ate until he was no longer hungry. He left after the meal and returned to his cousin, Raven.

"Cousin, where have you been all day?" Raven asked.

"Yonder. I walked along the seashore," Fox replied.

"While you were there, what did you do?" Raven asked.

"Nothing really! But I'm not hungry. I had a big meal."

Raven too was ready to leave to have a look. He wanted to find the place where his cousin had eaten so well. On his venture, he found the house. Raven was standing in front of the house when the same woman came out to greet him. She asked him the same question she had asked Fox, "How do I look? Am I a beautiful woman?"

"Ikii, you are ugly!" Raven replied.

Too bad! Raven was not as crafty as was told in other stories from way back. In all of the other stories he was a liar and more.

The woman did not invite Raven inside the house because of his "ikii" comment about her. After standing by the door waiting and waiting for a long time, Raven left and returned home. Poor guy, he didn't have anything to eat! He told his cousin that he hadn't had his meal and then asked his cousin how he managed to obtain his food.

Fox asked, "What did she ask you when you were at the door?"

Raven said, "The woman who was ugly asked me, 'How do I look? Am I a beautiful woman?' I said, 'Ikii! You are ugly!'"

Tricky fox laughed gleefully. As was characteristic of Fox, he didn't tell his cousin what to do if he happened to see this woman. Fox was crafty and had a scrumptious meal. Raven wasn't as crafty and didn't get any food to eat.

10

From Modernity to Self-Determination

Modernization arrived in Selawik as elsewhere. It occurred, however, at a different pace and in a different mode from that witnessed in more urbanized American settings. Being located far away in the Arctic and separated geographically from the Lower 48 by Canada, Alaska and Alaska Natives were adversely impacted by a particular phase of American political history at the time of the acquisition of Alaska and, in the case of Alaska Natives, also by the lack of political power and influence. As discussed in chapter 3, the earliest federal modernization efforts after the US acquisition of Alaska in 1867 reflected the administrative mindset and policies of the colonization and territorial expansion period. Early Western education arrived in Alaska hand-in-glove with Christianization to accommodate the government's financial and administrative conveniences. Natives met them with mixed reactions, followed by unanticipated cultural consequences. In Selawik, oral accounts tell about students being punished for speaking the Iñupiaq language of their parents. Iñupiaq dances were denigrated and demonized as the worship of the devil. The older generation who knew how to dance and enjoyed dancing were frowned upon by the church, and therefore the Iñupiaq art forms of music and dance were not passed on to the later generations. The teaching of dancing was only reversed in some villages in the region. Instead, Western music and musical instruments were introduced as the appropriate musical style. In these civilizing and missionizing efforts, Native cultural assimilation into American mainstream culture was prioritized. The concept of free exercise of religion, as mandated by the US Constitution, was overlooked in

https://doi.org/10.5876/9781646426065.c010

order to spread Christian civilization as efficiently and widely as possible through a process by which different missionary societies were assigned exclusive concessions to different parts of Alaska. The California Friends were given Northwest Alaska. It was not until much later that other Christian denominations made their appearance. In the 1960s, the Iñupiaq activist movement to attain rights and respect as the original people of the land, self-determination, and reclaiming the loss of many aspects of their cultural heritages and Iñupiaq identity became meaningful issues.

In Selawik, the pace of modernity accelerated after Senator Edward Kennedy's visit to Alaska in 1969, when he echoed his older brother John's concern, expressed nearly a decade earlier, that Alaska Natives were living in substandard traditional houses. Senator Kennedy's comments assisted in advancing proposals already being formulated by BIA-HUD Programs to introduce modern government housing into the villages, which ultimately resulted in the Housing and Community Development Act of 1977.

Prefabricated houses were brought into Selawik on barges in August 1970 and were set up in a line south of the school. While well intended and much appreciated, the houses, painted in different colors, sat on triangular supports on wooden pilings two feet above the ground, a design to keep the permafrost underneath from melting. Unfortunately, possibly through an oversight of architects unfamiliar with Arctic subzero temperatures and windswept tundra terrain, the space between the frozen ground and the living floors was not enclosed. Thus the inadequately insulated floors were constantly swept by strong freezing winds that chilled the floors. Also, the houses were designed to be entered directly from the outside without the benefit of a functional enclosed storm shed, known locally as the *qanisaq*, which helped insulate houses. Entering a house, one was met with a frigid blast that condensed into an apron of ice that covered the floor. Many occupants subsequently lived all winter in a frosted living space. And, due to the unstable foundation on top of the permafrost, the houses swayed in strong tundra winds until the blizzards buried the lower parts of the houses in snow. Each house had a modern bathroom, but running water was a project left to be developed—sometime in the future. In 1977, a second set of nineteen improved government houses corrected many of these deficiencies. But even with these improvements, not every family moved into the new housing; many old people preferred to stay in their old, warmer, semisubterranean sod houses. Another architectural drawback of the new houses was their inconvenient location far from the river, a requirement necessitated by the planned future development of a village water and sewage disposal system. To process their fish hauled in by boat from the fish camps or other netting sites, women found it more convenient to return to their old home sites to do the fish cutting before carrying the fish up to drying racks near their new houses.

The new housing changed the settlement pattern of the school side of the village. With the sixteen additional houses put in behind the first set of thirteen houses, Selawik, formerly marked by riverfront houses, took on the appearance of a planned gridlike village with rows of houses behind the original riverfront houses. Instead of roads, boardwalks spanning the wet muskeg ran in front of these houses.

Selawik village, linked to the outside world not by roads but by boat, snowmobile, and airplane, had exceedingly limited income-paying occupations. In 1968, only the mayor, the postmaster, a nurse aide, two Native teacher aides, two cooks, and the school custodian held salaried occupations. The education personnel—the Euro-American principal and three teachers—came in from the outside. The continuity and retention of the school teaching staff were always problems, as teachers from the outside normally relocated after a few years. In 1976, the State of Alaska had lost the schooling discrimination court case, *Hootch v Alaska State-Operated School System*, which gave the right to high school education under the State of Alaska School system to Alaska villages with eight or more high school-age students (Hirshberg and Sharp 2005). The new education mandate and working cooperation between Grant Ballot of the Selawik School Board and school principal James Ede led to a new chapter in Selawik educational history. Selawik school curriculum was extended to include high school programming and brought in additional high school buildings and increased the number of teachers to eight. Eight teachers were teaching. Selawikers felt more at ease as their high-school-age children did not need to venture outside to US Bureau of Indian Affairs boarding schools, where many of them had had uneasy times.

Few Selawikers attended college. A large number of these first-year college students returned home disappointed and did not complete their college education as intended.

James Ede's philosophy of liberal education brought about bilingual and bicultural education to Selawik in 1972, integrating the teaching of Iñupiaq language and culture into the formal school curriculum as part of the Eskimo Culture program of Alaska's Department of Education. He had enrolled Selawik as one of the first three state-operated village schools, along with Buckland and Noatak, to participate in the initial stage of the program. The initiative created additional local Native teaching positions of Iñupiaq language and culture. In Selawik, one instructor was responsible for teaching in the lower-grade level and the other in the higher-grade level. The initial stage of teaching was difficult since no one was formally trained as an Iñupiaq language instructor—and there were no Iñupiaq textbooks to provide guidance. A standardized Romanized script for writing Iñupiaq was not yet in place, so instructors had to be innovative, starting from scratch. Wanni, who had studied two foreign languages, was recruited to tutor one inexperienced elderly Iñupiaq teacher on how to teach a language class and how to prepare her day-to-day lesson plan.

Selawikers voted to become a first-class city in 1976. The move provided them with a larger city budget and more independent administrative decisions about their own community developments. Multiple community and educational projects were initiated under the authority of the City Council. James Ede was elected president of the council to oversee the implementation of several village initiatives. The established Selawik High School program in 1976 attracted all the eighth-grade graduates into the program and also brought in a number of high school students from Buckland and Kobuk River villages that did not yet have their own high schools. Selawik can be recorded as being in the forefront of this local high school movement in the region. It marked the end of the earlier education model of sending students far away to the BIA high schools outside.

Another community development project improved the quality of life. Within the village it was ironic that, with the oil drilling in Alaska of the 1970s, the costs of boat gasoline and home heating oil were exorbitant in Selawik and the Kobuk villages—over $8 a gallon compared to the Lower 48's prices around $2 at the time. Every year Selawik residents worried about the timely transport of the oil by barge before the freeze-up. To ensure a sufficient supply of home heating oil during the long, frigid winter, an oil storage facility was built and a community office of Alaska Village Electric Cooperative, created in 1968, set up. The larger city operating budget enabled another construction project that vastly improved living conditions. Boardwalks that used to exist only in front of the school area were extended throughout the whole village to eliminate wet, slippery dirt paths during the spring thaw. Selawik's first bridge was later constructed to connect the school side of the Selawik River to the island. This project, later expanded to include a bridge from the island to the air strip on the Siktaavik side, solved the danger of crossing the river before freeze-up and during the spring thaws that used to lead to school truancy. A byproduct of the high school construction was a community laundromat and shower facility built from leftover construction materials. Women with no running water in their houses were happy that they were no longer burdened with having to haul water up from the river to do their laundry or to dry their wet laundry "Selawik-style" in winter, that is, to first let it freeze on an outside clothesline, then knock off the ice before bringing clothes inside to hang over the hot stove to dry. The laundromat was a boon, especially for families returning home from their spring and summer fish camps with a huge load of dirty laundry.

The school also had a "go green" experiment with a hothouse that distributed saplings to villagers. Many houses that we visited during that period had houseplants and other plants like avocado plants inside the house.

Another first in Selawik history occurred during this period: the city funded an archaeological field school for high school students to acquaint them with the fact that their own cultural history was metaphorically in their own backyard. In the summer of 1976, Douglas was invited to direct the two-week field school at Fox River in which eight students participated. The positive learning experience led to Douglas and Wanni being invited to teach another field school in 1981. The curriculum of the second field school was expanded from a local archaeology excavation to include the study of oral history and museology. Another step in a more culturally responsive high school curriculum was the introduction of Julie Ede's business class. To train students who might aspire to a business career, an empty building on the school side of the river was converted into a village café named The Northern Lights, which gave students hands-on experience at running a small hamburger, hot dog, and soft drinks café. The food and coffee was cooked and served by students with welcoming smiles.

In 1977, Selawik reverted to its former status as a second-class city, and the Selawik School went under the jurisdiction of the Northwest Arctic School District.

IÑUPIAQ SELF-DETERMINATION

Edward W. Said (1994), a noted critic of colonialism and imperialism, offered perceptive political views for examining culture and cultural contention and the resistance responses of the colonized Indigenous:

> Culture is a sort of theatre where various political and ideological causes engage one another . . . Culture can be even a battle ground on which causes expose themselves to the light of day and contend with one another. (xiii)

> Opposition to a dominant structure arises out of a perceived, perhaps even militant awareness on the part of individuals and groups outside and inside it that, for example, certain of its politics are wrong. (240)

In the 1960s, at the beginning of Alaska statehood, the Iñupiat of Northwest Alaska responded to what they viewed as wrong. To put the Iñupiat ("the People") on a new path, a group of young Iñupiaq activists worked together to bring back regional control and pride in Iñupiaq culture. At the core of Iñupiaq culture they identified seventeen traditional values, termed "Inupiat Ilitqusait," which served as a mandate for creating Iñupiaq-conscious institutions. "Ilitqusait" refers to what makes Iñupiat who they are. Leaders of the Inupiat Ilitqusait movement felt strongly that Iñupiaq identity requires life to be lived with dignity and respect. Within the two cultural worlds that Iñupiat have to mediate, the Western cultural world can be integrated without having to abandon what is valuable in the Iñupiaq world. John Schaeffer Jr. of Kotzebue, the first Iñupiaq two-star general in the Alaska Army National Guard and Commissioner of the Alaska Department of Military and Veterans Affairs, assisted in opening many doors to Iñupiaq political, economic, and social empowerment. The Northwest Arctic Native Association (NANA) was established in 1972, as part of the Alaska Native Claims Settlement Act (ANCSA), to act as trustee of the Northwest Alaska region and to administer economic development within it. Schaeffer served as NANA's first president. The Maniilaq Association was established as a nonprofit for health and social services. It is named after Maniilaq, the well-known "Eskimo Prophet," who was born on the upper Kobuk in the early 1800s.

When the Canadian Tech Resources mining company gained a mining contract in partnership with NANA to mine zinc, lead, and silver in Northwest Alaska at a location known as the Red Dog Mine, the terms of the agreement under Schaeffer's proactive guidance required that 60 percent of the workers be local Natives. In this natural resource development strategy, regional control and employment opportunities for local Natives were integrated into the support for traditional subsistence activities by establishing a work shift of two weeks on and two weeks off, so that the workers could return to their home villages to hunt and fish.

The proposed ANCSA legislation also gave Schaeffer and another young leader, Willie Hensley, opportunities to implement their Iñupiaq self-determination directive. Public hearings soliciting villagers' opinions on the bill were held in different villages. The two-day hearing in Selawik, which Grant Ballot officiated on March 6–7, 1972, was well attended; we also were present to observe.

At the Selawik meeting, John Schaeffer, Willie Hensley, Robert Newlin Sr., and Willie Godwin Jr. took turns presenting their case for the settlement to Selawik villagers, advocating for Iñupiaq Native rights, and soliciting discussion of community problems that ought to be addressed in provisions of the bill relevant to Northwest Alaska residents. A videotape titled "You Are Getting Rich on My Land" gave a rationale as to why NANA was fighting for the 2 percent royalties from the oil drilling corporations in Alaska. A movie shown, *Sky River: An Experiment in Change*, had an Iñupiaq father expressing disappointment at his daughter's high school education outside in a BIA school, costing her formative years learning traditional Iñupiaq ways in her home village. Selawik villagers participated actively in the hearing, asking for more livable housing.

In discussions of the proposed bill, Selawik residents requested that twenty-two historic settlements, graveyard sites, and a former reindeer breeding ground be included in the Selawik list, under provisions of Section 14(h) of ANCSA. It was a critical regional meeting. Similar to what William Schneider reported for the Athabaskan village of Chalkyitsik (Schneider 1986:119), what would be implemented through ANCSA was an issue of vital concern to Native leaders who were called upon to lead and make decisions.

As events evolved, the US National Park Service asked us to conduct a baseline study of Native subsistence issues related to the proposed Kobuk Valley National Monument (later upgraded to a National Park). The research, undertaken in 1974–1975 by Douglas D. Anderson, Ray Bane, Richard K. Nelson, Wanni W. Anderson, and Nita Sheldon, resulted in a report to the National Park Service titled *Kuuvangmiut Subsistence: Traditional Eskimo Life in the Latter Twentieth Century* (D. Anderson et al. 1977). NANA ended up sharing funding for the publication of the revised report (D. Anderson et al. 1998). As part of this study, several areas were identified as ancient ancestral settlements and grave sites, which, under provisions of Section 14(h), helped secure them as set-asides for historical preservation.

Since the Selawik River system was legislated to be under the jurisdiction of the US Fish and Wildlife Service, Selawik was not a part of the NPS subsistence study. In Selawik, VISTA volunteers helped Selawikers—as they did for residents of other villages in the region—register their claims for Native allotments with the Bureau of Land Management, but no detailed study of human and natural resources that might have impacted the findings was carried out for Selawik.

In 1981, Selawik participated in a NANA community development project to experiment with the development of a summer potato farm, the Spud Farm, north of the village, so that the villagers could rely on a harvest from their own local crops instead of having to buy from outside at a higher cost. Since the land to be developed was on NANA lands, Douglas was brought in as the archaeologist to conduct a site survey to ensure no archaeological sites might be destroyed by the farming.

To redress the loss of many elements of Iñupiaq culture, another humanitarian organization, the Aqqaluk Trust, founded in honor of former NANA president Robert Aqqaluk Newlin Sr., continued to work side-by-side with NANA. Its emphasis is on culture, language, and education: "When an Iñupiaq person becomes educated and understands his identity, he can play a vital role and become a leader" (Newlin's mimeographed speech presented to the participants at the Spirit Program, 1981). Newlin felt that as a child educated in the strictly Western school education curriculum, he was deprived of learning traditional Iñupiaq culture. The trust organizes the annual summer culture camp, where schoolchildren of different age groups are brought together for a week at Camp Sivuniiġvik, near Noorvik, on the Kobuk River to learn about Iñupiaq traditional values, self-respect, and respect for the environment. Selawik schoolchildren signed up to participate in the program every summer, and a number of Selawik women worked as camp counselors and cooks. The organization has expanded to become the local educational foundation in support of higher education for Iñupiat who aspire to advanced education in college or in vocational institutions.

IÑUPIAQ LANGUAGE

Iñupiaq language, a significant marker of Iñupiaq cultural identity, was affected from the very founding of Selawik village. The consequences of the national policy enforced by the teachers' strict enforcement of "No Iñupiaq Spoken," discussed in chapter 3, was far-reaching and clearly visible two generations later. In 1968, when we first arrived in the village, we learned that only the oldest generation had full command of their mother tongue. Our observation was later supported by an official survey in 2005 showing that only 14 percent of the Iñupiat in the region had fluency in understanding Iñupiaq.

During the early years of the Iñupiaq self-determination movement of the 1980s, reclaiming the Iñupiaq language was a priority. In 1998, in Kotzebue, the headquarters of NANA, Tarruq Peter Schaeffer founded Nikaichuat Ilisaqviat ("a place to learn that anything is possible"), as an independent Iñupiaq language and culture immersion school for three-to-six-year-olds. NANA provided the school building, and funding came from the cooperation of four organizations: NANA, Maniilaq, the Northwest Arctic Borough, and the Kotzebue Indian Reorganization Act Office. The school's mission was to instill the dignity of Iñupiaq identity through the learning of Iñupiaq language and culture from early childhood (Oakley 2001).

The 1979 publication of *Kaniqsisautit Uqayusragnikun* (Kobuk Iñupiat Junior Dictionary) (Sun et al. 1979), developed by the staff of the National Bilingual Materials Development Center, made great strides toward standardizing written Iñupiaq. It provided much-needed critical guidance for teachers of Iñupiaq in the eleven village schools in the Northwest Arctic region.

In 1975, Maniilaq spearheaded the collection of traditional knowledge from elders. A number of these Iñupiaq culture bearers were later brought together in Elders Conferences from 1976 to 1983 to talk about traditional lifeways, history, and the stories in their repertoires. "The elders were made to feel that their knowledge and experiences were indeed valuable" (Lee, Sampson, and Tennant 1989:ix). Narratives recorded at the Elders Conference in 1976, 1977, and 1978 became resource materials for the first bilingual book, *Unipchaallu Uqaaqtuallu: Legends and Stories* (Loon, Newlin, and Sampson 1979–1980). Other narratives recorded at the conferences were later published as the three-volume bilingual series *Lore of the Iñupiat: The Elders Speak: Uqaaqtuanich Inupiat* (Lee, Sampson, and Tennant 1989; Lee et al. 1990; Lee, Sampson, and Tennant 1992). For the first time, textbooks were specifically produced for school instruction of Iñupiaq language and culture class.

Figure 10.1. Ruthie Sampson and Wanni working on the manuscript of *Folktales of the Riverine and Coastal Iñupiat*, 2002.

Selawik actively participated in the movement. Nora Norton told her stories, Nellie Russell talked about bear hunting, Daniel Foster told stories and talked about hunger and survival, and Elmer and Effie Ballot provided glimpses into the Selawik past.

Ruthie Tatqaviñ Sampson of Selawik also served as the first coordinator of the bilingual and bicultural program of the Northwest Arctic School District. The program grew under her leadership. One Selawik mother proudly proclaimed, "My children know more Iñupiaq than I do." Sampson later worked with her assistants to edit another bilingual book, *Qayaqtauginnaqtuaq (Qayaq: The Magical Traveler)* (Lee, Sampson, and Tennant 1991), from a taped legend told in one of the Elders Conferences. Sampson's next project was with Robert Gal, Kotzebue-based archaeologist of the Alaska National Park Service, which resulted in the publication of *Kuuvangmiut Subsistence: Traditional Eskimo Life in the Latter Twentieth Century* (D. Anderson et al. 1998) as a textbook. Sampson again served as Iñupiaq editor of another bilingual textbook, *Folktales of the Riverine and Coastal Iñupiat: Unipchallu Uqaaqtuallu Kuunmiuninlu Tagiugmiuninlu* (W. Anderson and Sampson 2003) for the schools in the Northwest Arctic School District (figure 10.1).

National policies enacted during different US presidencies had varying impacts on Alaska Native rural communities. The first setback to the enriching Iñupiaq teaching program occurred in 2002, with President George W. Bush's "No Child Left Behind" educational policy in which English reading and math were prioritized nationally as the yardstick for measuring students' academic achievement. No new federal funding was for teaching Iñupiaq, and previously allocated funding, essential for the growth of bilingual and bicultural programs in the Northwest Arctic School District, was diverted. This underscored once again that the government's top-down decisions often left no room for Native needs or wishes.

NANA later stepped in to assist in the Iñupiaq language recovery efforts. With Sampson as the Iñupiaq linguist, the organization developed an Iñupiaq interactive language learning program on a CD-ROM that can be accessed online. On the college level, the Chukchi Community College, a branch of the University of Alaska system in Kotzebue since 1978, offered three levels of Iñupiaq language courses, beginning, intermediate, and advanced, with Sampson serving as a long-distance instructor from her retirement village in Shungnak until she passed away. The new generation of Iñupiat has opportunities that their parents never had.

Relative to other Iñupiaq villages on the coast and on the Kobuk River, Selawik is unique as a village on the tundra with its specific environmental characteristics and past history. As it moved into the twenty-first century, the village continued to be actively participate in NANA initiatives. Selawik representatives sit on the boards of directors of NANA, Maniilaq, and the Aqqaluk Trust. The inter-village connection between the Siilaviŋmiut and the Kuuvaŋmiut remain close through existing kinship ties and new marital bonds of young couples from the new generation. The 2022 census enumerated the growth of Selawik population to be 816 people, the second-largest Iñupiaq community after Kotzebue. The Selawik School, renamed the Davis-Ramoth Memorial School after village leaders Lloyd Davis and Edward Ramoth, is thriving. As of 2022, twenty teachers served a student body of 272. Selawik still has no streets, only walking paths covered by boardwalks. The federal pressure to put every household on a street address led the school to be officially listed as sitting on Musk Ox Parkway. Across the river on Akuliĝaq Island, the main boardwalk running in front of the Friends Church and Rotman's Store now bears the Riverside Street postal address.

Through pumping up water from the Selawik River, running water has finally come to houses in the village, although residents have to contend with occasional frozen water pipes during the winter's subzero temperatures. The two bridges built over the two channels of the Selawik River have made life and social interactional contacts much easier for residents. When we first arrived in Selawik in 1968, we were thrilled at the sight of children as young as seven or eight years old running outboard motorboats or rowing across the river. On our last visit in 2012, a mother complained that children of the new generation no longer know how to row. Instead, we were greeted by the sight of an eight-year-old girl on a four-wheeler driving by on the island's busy boardwalk (figure 10.2). We heard an irate grandfather who was going to a grocery store calling on his CB radio for his granddaughter

Figure 10.2. One of the many boardwalks that run through Selawik.

to immediately bring back his Honda four-wheeler. A new lingo was born as the young added the in-phrase "I Honda . . ." in addition to "I sno-go . . ."

By 2000, the Siktaavik, or airport side of the Selawik River had expanded from just two family homes in 1971 to seven houses. It was still the least populated side of the village. The visual landscape of the village has drastically transformed the school side. Dubbed "Tube City" by some outsiders, corrugated insulation tubes for the electric and television lines and water pipes snake their way aboveground from house to house. The utility layout was constrained by the hard, concrete-like permafrost ground of the tundra, which made burying them out of sight underground beyond budgetary limits, as well as too problematic to dig through should repairs be needed in winter.

IÑUPIAT OF THE SII

Fish remain plentiful in the Sii. Although store-bought foods have become integral parts of the daily diet, a number of the new generation of women have picked up their mothers' summer fishing and processing activities to maintain a supply of the traditional Iñupiaq food that they still love. Many men have responded to the challenge of the traditional Iñupiaq subsistence lifeways and matured as skilled hunters bringing in the familiar meat diet. Within families, babies continue to be much cherished. Many families continue to exchange babies, as they did in the past, to have the joy of having children in the house after their own children have grown up. Children continue to be a significant loving bond in their lives. The interfacing of the traditional with the modern is visible in the village basketball team, the Selawik Wolves, which has evolved to become the symbolic mascot of the Davis-Ramoth Memorial School. The school's website advertises the sale of team T-shirts and caps. Recently, through Maniilaq and its health network, a new, more spacious, and better-equipped health clinic on the island has replaced the former smaller health clinic on the school side of the river.

Selawik as village has stood over a century. The construction of boardwalks throughout the village has remedied a former drawback, the wet, muddy ground after the spring thaw. Its location along the stretch of land on the banks of the Sii River and Akuliġaq Island has allowed the village settlement to stretch out along four riverbanks and facilitated viable subsistence fishing activities. Being the only village on the Sii has given it another advantage: it has enabled Selawikers to maintain territorial autonomy, not having to contend with overlapping village subsistence boundaries and interests, as some villagers on the Kobuk River experience. Essential to the Selawik ethos is the villagers' strong sense of community. Learning about places along the Sii where the fish are bountiful, where herds of caribou migrate by, and where their grandparents used to have their settlements and camps have fortified and deepened their sense of their home. It strengthens and sustains their senses of belonging and identity. In the view of Selawikers, the ongoing culture change will continue to demand their adaptive mindset and mediated strategies and responses. Like their forefathers, they have retained their culture of resiliency, skilled at adapting to new changes and new technologies that might improve their lives. An Iñupiaq who knows how to repair a broken boat motor or snowmobile without benefit of a formal mechanic course is quintessentially a true Iñupiaq. Within the Northwest Arctic region, their spatial and social connectedness to the nearest village Noorvik on the Kobuk River is as strong as in the past. Politically, they stand firmly behind NANA, Maniilaq Association, and the Aqqaluk Trust in their proactive efforts on behalf of the Iñupiat. They are Iñupiat, the Iñupiat of the Sii River, the Siilaviŋmiut.

As the Sii River continues to flow, a significant part of village life, to be bilingual and bicultural, living as Iñupiat with integrity and dignity and making the right decisions for the future path, continues to pose critical challenges.

Appendix 1

Selawik High School Students' Journals of the 1981 Archaeology and Oral History Field School

The Selawik high school students who participated in the 1981 archaeology and oral history field school were George Foster, Ben Ramoth, Beverly Davis, Martha Norton (Tukka), Marvin (Ricky) Henry, Richard Berry, and Peggy Ramoth. As a way of teaching students how anthropologists record their data in their research fieldnotes, students were instructed to keep daily journals. Below are examples of the journals of two students, Richard Berry and Beverly Davis. The excerpts are reprinted as written by the students, except in certain sentences where they have been lightly edited for clarity.

RICHARD BERRY'S JOURNAL
JUNE 8–81

- archaeology regulations
- history of Selawik
- surveying techniques
- excavation
- write up archaeology report
  - oral history
  - write a book on the history of Selawik

https://doi.org/10.5876/9781646426065.c011

Selawik was first founded in 1908. People from up the river had to go to school here. Selawik is 75 years old. Selawik people were living about 20 miles upriver when this teacher came and started school here and the young people had to go to school. That's how Selawik grew here instead of upriver.

Ben Ramoth, Marvin Berry, Martha Norton, Beverly Davis, Peggy Ramoth and I started to clear the old igloo on the north side of Selawik. It was probably built in the early 1900s or 1890? Anyway we cleared the place in one day and that same day Paul Ballot who is about 80 years old came to us and started to talk about early Selawik. He said that a white man came to Selawik in 1908 and started a school. Also he was a missionary. So the people from up the river came here to school. There were not too many students at that time. The white man got logs from some place and built the school. Paul Ballot said his Mom and Dad were one of the first to attend school. Paul Ballot himself was scared of the white man then but today he talked to a lot of white people. He also told us about the history of early Selawik. He told us when he was a little boy, the 5 lbs sugar cost 60 cents and coffee $1.00. And other more things I didn't catch. And also he said something about Robert and Carrie Samms coming to Selawik to teach the people of Selawik. He said the west and the east banks of Selawik had lots of willows then and the people cut them and made their houses and igloos. He also told us about a store that was built around Selawik.

Second Day

Ben Ramoth, Martha Norton, Ricky Henry, Peggy Ramoth, Beverly Davis, Marvin Berry and I, Richard Berry, started to dig around the igloo and took off sod blocks and found pieces of wood and some charcoal.

Second day of work. Grant Ballot came to visit us and said that when he was a boy he could throw (a stone) across the Nigraq and from the Nigraq to the island. He said the river was very narrow then and during these years, there has been a lot of erosion.

Fourth Day

We dug and found some fish and sinkers. I found an old fishhook made of ivory, and we found old beads and a bone that was from a prehistoric mammoth. Peggy Ramoth found two suspender snaps and a bone that looks like an earring or a fishhook. Someone found a dog chain. Ben Ramoth found that.

At noon Ben Ramoth, Martha Norton and I went to interview Minnie Kalhok, Ray Skin and Johnny Foster. Minnie Kalhok was sleeping, so we went to Ray Skin and he showed us some old pictures. We went to Johnny Foster who told us that Lulu's husband used to run to school from the island near the dumps. There were other people who had to do that. Ray Skin said that Joe Foxglove was a reindeer herder, and Richard Jones and Charlie Smith (too). Ray Skin showed us a picture of Joe Foxglove going to his reindeer camp about 40 miles toward Buckland.

Fifth Day, June 13, 1981

We were all on time to start digging the artifacts and we dug and found some dog chain links. I found an old stone lamp and nails and pieces of birch bark and Marvin found a muskrat that was just skinned and Tukka found a wooden spoon for picking berries or for cooking soup. Marvin and Beverly found some beads and Tukka found a piece of wood that has a sharp point in the end. We don't know what it is. We also found some nails and some fish net sinkers.

At noon Peggy, Ben and I went to interview Leonor Skin and she said that long ago Joe Foxglove and Charlie Smith and Richard Jones used to run to school from the dump. We started back to work. That's all.

Sixth Day

When we all got to the place, it was very muddy because of the rain. It was very wet. Anyway we dug and I found a couple of nails and a button that was from a soldier coat from World War I jacket or coat. Tukka found a bead, a very small one. Ben Foxglove found a big log that has lots of nails sticking out from it. Ricky found birch wedge. Peggy found nothing. Ben Ramoth found some glass and Beverly found nothing. Marvin found some birch wood pieces. Then it was lunch time.

Oh, Ben found a round, copper piece that had a hole in it. It was about the size of a silver dollar.

BEVERLY DAVIS'S JOURNAL

June 8, 1981, Monday

We started working estimating at 9.30, at the high school. Doug talked to us about the history of Selawik, how it got bigger, how they lived in igloos. They were founded in 1908. Now Selawik is about 73 years old. It was founded around 1908.

Archaeology Project:

- history of Selawik
- journal

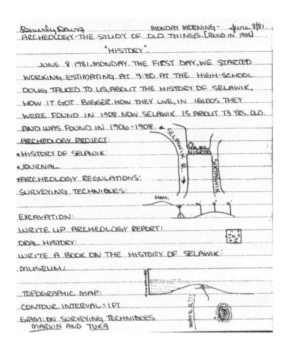

Figure A1.1. A page from a Selawik High School student's 1981 archeology and oral history field school journal.

- archaeology regulations, surveying techniques
- excavation
- write up archaeology report
- oral history
- write a book on the history of Selawik
- museum

Monday Afternoon

We started off taking all the grass off the Native igloo and some of the willows. After that we had a break. Paul Ballot came to visit us and talked about the history of Selawik. He said there was this guy who owned a store there and Robert and Carrie Samms who lived there. It was a nice day. Hot.

June 9, 1981, Tuesday

Johnny Norton took us to work. We started working on taking off some pieces of mud off. Then Tuka found a piece of log that was cut a long time ago and Richard found a piece of lead, then he measured it and wrote it down on the map. Then I found a pole and Doug told me to leave it there for later on.

Today's weather is much colder than yesterday's weather at 10.30. Doug told us to drink juice for 15 minutes and to write on our papers for another 15 minutes. Richard told us he saw another house way up there and Doug said he might go up to check it.

Ricky Henry, our new employee (student), has come to help us work. It was a great pleasure that now there are seven of us working there. There is supposed to be nine of us but two didn't show up, Miranda Cleveland and Bryant Tikik. Bryant used to work with Doug and Wanni when he was in school.

Today a boat came by itself because its hook came off and it floated here to where we are working. It is a small boat. It is about 15–20 ft.

Paul Ballot told us where his parents lived and where he lived. He said his house was flooded by the water but they made another house at another spot and they tore the old house down. He didn't know about white men too much. But he told us about the missionaries.

Today we all had lunch here at Doug's and Wanni's place. We ate sandwiches, drank juice, and ate fruit. After that we started digging deeper. Then Grant Ballot came here to visit us (Paul Ballot's son). While we were working he talked to Doug that "when he was young and small" the land over there was narrow and he used to throw rocks from across the land (bank) to another land (bank). He stayed here for about 5–10 minutes with Steve, his wife's son. After he left my older sister and her friend Jimmy and Norma drop by and she gave me a can of pop (root beer). I had to cool it off because it was in the sun. In fact the sun is right above us where we are digging.

JUNE 10, 1981

We started working estimating at 9.20. Later we started digging and Doug told us we all can go to check if there is another house way over there. We went all the way to another river and we left Wanni. And Peggy found a bird nest near the graves. After all that walk, we started working again. And after we worked we had lunch. At the same time Emma Norton, Tukka's mother, brought some food here for us. Marvin found a busted egg that wasn't hatched. And Tukka found a robin nest, but it didn't lay its eggs. We went back to work while Emma was still here watching what we were doing. Then the other four (students) went interviewing with Wanni and Emma.

Later on, me, Ricky and Peggy kept on working. Ricky found a shot gun shell and I found a nail. Doug found a cloth and birch wood. Then we had a break for 15 minutes and another break for writing in our journals.

JUNE 11, 1981, TUESDAY MORNING

Me and Peggy went to the boat and waited for Johnny Norton, our boatman, but he didn't show up and Tukka came to join us. Later on Johnny finally showed up. He said to us, "I forgot about you fellas." He said to Tukka "Tukka, you'll scold me for that?" That made us laugh.

This morning Peggy found a small shell and Ricky found a dog snap by the woods.

JUNE 12, 1981

Yesterday after we ate lunch, me, Peggy and Ricky and Wanni went to see Topsy (Ramoth) to interview, but she wasn't interested. Next we went to see Sarah Goode and she was interested and I had to talk to her. After we were done we went to the store and got some food. We went back to Richard Jones and he told us that he went to school with Kitty Foster and Minnie Kalhok and he remembered Joe Lee Sickles. Yesterday Richard Jones told us they used to play with a lot of boys and they used to eat reindeer and some of the teachers lunched.

Yesterday morning Barb came to visit and look at of the artifacts we found. Later on a group from Fairbanks that stayed with Oran also came to visit. They all had canoes. Then it was lunch time. I followed Wanni to their house to help her with fixing the food and the Fairbanks group ate with us. After a while Ricky and Richard asked Barb if they can try their canoe and it was alright. Ben found and got a fish which me and Peggy cut up and hang on the racks. When me and Peggy were done, I and she went on the canoe. We went all the way to the other stop. Tukka, Richard, Ben, Marvin went interviewing.

JUNE 13, 1981, SATURDAY

This morning I thought we weren't gonna work and I overslept. Peggy woke me up and then we worked on our journal. I was late because they didn't tell me I had to work.

This afternoon after lunch, Peggy, Ben, Richard and Wanni went to Arthur and Leonora to interview and then they all went to Mary Knox's place. Then they tried going to Lucy's but she wasn't there. After they left, we found some nails, beads to make a net and a wooden spoon, Cloth to hold suspenders, bones. We had a break and we ate some pop-tarts and the other group came. We wrote on our journals.

JUNE 15, 1981, MONDAY

This morning we all started digging and we didn't find anything for a long time because it had water on the mud from the rain or it must have got too soft and melted.

It was 10.30 and we had a break. Johnny came with Marvin and later on Ben found a round thing that has a hole. And he found seal skin and a glass. Marvin found a wire that was lost the other day.

As time went on we kept on digging. Me, Tukka, Wanni and Peggy went to go see Lucy Smith but she wasn't interested. We went back, got the key and went to Wanni's place and made some lunch. When we were coming back Grant and his wife and their kids came by and Dorcas hung her fishes. They ate some sandwiches with us. They stayed here for about ½ an hour. Richard got his rod and fished for awhile, then Marvin, then me. I had 2 fishes but I let them go. Tukka tried twice.

1.00 came. We started writing on our journals and after a while we will go interviewing Kitty Foster if she isn't busy. Or we will go to check on Minnie Kalhok.

Yesterday before we quit working at Nigraq we covered the ground with the sod we took off and Doug told us to go to work at the gym. Today the 16th of June, we placed all the artifacts we found and straightened them, nut and all. We had a break. Wanni gave us some juice and gum and the break was over. We worked until 12.00 and then worked on our journals about today's work.

Appendix 2

Fish Counts of Two Fisherwomen

Clara Ballot and Lenora Skin

Clara Ballot, 1977, Net fishing site at Sisavik with two nets

Date	Whitefish	Pike	Shee	Mud shark	Extenuating circumstances
Jun 15	5	30			
Jun 16	15	24			
Jun 17	84	34	17	2	
Jun 18	20	5			
Jun 19					
Jun 20	13	30			
Jun 21	24	23			
Jun 22–24					death in village
Jun 25	9	43	1		
Jun 26					church day
Jun 27	21	34			
Jun 28					too windy
Jun 29	25	41			
Jun 30					too windy
Jul 1					too windy
Jul 2	30	48			

continued on next page

https://doi.org/10.5876/9781646426065.c012

Clara Ballot—*continued*

Date	Whitefish	Pike	Shee	Mud shark	Extenuating circumstances
Jul 3					church day
Jul 4	28	40			
Jul 5	22	32			
Jul 6	33	25			
Jul 8	29	29			
Jul 11	17	19			
Jul 12	4	35			
Jul 13	5	39			
Jul 28	168				
Jul 29	393				
Aug 11	183				
Aug 12	303				
Aug 15	40				
Aug 22	200				
Aug 25	421				
Oct 1	15	5	2	2	
Oct 3	32	7		1	
Oct 4	11	1			
Oct 5	18	4	3		
Oct 6	29	6	1	1	
Oct 7	16	9	1		
Oct 8	10	7	5		
Oct 10	28	9	9		
Oct 11	19	4	3		
Oct 12	19	11	6	1	
Oct 13	28	19	4		
Oct 16	23	20	4		
Oct 17	19	8		2	
Oct 19	36	30		10	
Oct 21	24	17		5	
Oct 22	16	14	1	3	
Oct 23	8	7			

continued on next page

Clara Ballot—*continued*

Date	Whitefish	Pike	Shee	Mud shark	Extenuating circumstances
Oct 24	34	10	3	3	
Oct 25	10	14		3	
Oct 26	6	4	1		
Total	2,493	737	61	33	

Lenora Skin, September and October 1972, with 2 nets

Date	Whitefish	Pike	Shee	Mud shark	Ikkuiyiq	Extenuating circumstances
Sep 4	9	6	2	2	16	
Sep 5	20	5			10	
Sep 6	10	2	1	2	9	
Sep 7	5	3			6	
Sep 8	6	4			5	
Sep 9	4	5		1	8	
Sep 10	2	4			7	
Sep 11	7	7	1		20	
Sep 12	8	4	1	2	11	
Sep 13	5	2			12	
Sep 14	3	1			5	
Sep 15	6	4			4	
Sep 16	9	2			9	
Sep 17	2	3			6	
Sep 18	4	6			7	
Sep 19	5	2			8	
Sep 20	2	4			9	
Sep 21	4	4			11	
Sep 22	5	3			8	
Sep 23	2	1			6	
Sep 24	6	2			4	
Sep 25	3	5			7	
Sep 26	4	6			9	
Sep 27	2	2			10	

continued on next page

Lenora Skin—*continued*

Date	Whitefish	Pike	Shee	Mud shark	Ikkuiyiq	Extenuating circumstances
Sep 28	3	1			6	
Sep 29	8	6				
Oct 1	20	2			6	
Oct 3	21	3			2	
Oct 4	25	5			1	
Oct 5	15	4			7	
Oct 6	27	2			4	
Oct 7	29	4			9	
Oct 8	14	3			6	
Oct 9						church day
Oct 10	30	2			10	
Oct 11	23	3			5	
Oct 12	14	2			6	
Oct 13	12	4			8	
Oct 14	10	2			4	
Oct 15	17	4			5	
Oct 16						church day
Oct 17	11	5			6	
Oct 18	24	3			8	
Oct 19	20	2			4	
Oct 20	17	1			3	
Oct 21	16	2			6	
Oct 22	18	3			4	
Oct 23						church day
Oct 24	20	2			5	
Oct 25	15	3			6	
Oct 26	17	4			7	
Oct 27	12	2			2	
Oct 28	30	2			5	
Oct 29	25	3			9	
Oct 30						church day
Oct 31	21	5			8	
Total	647	171	5	7	359	

Appendix 3

1979 Selawik Christmas Program

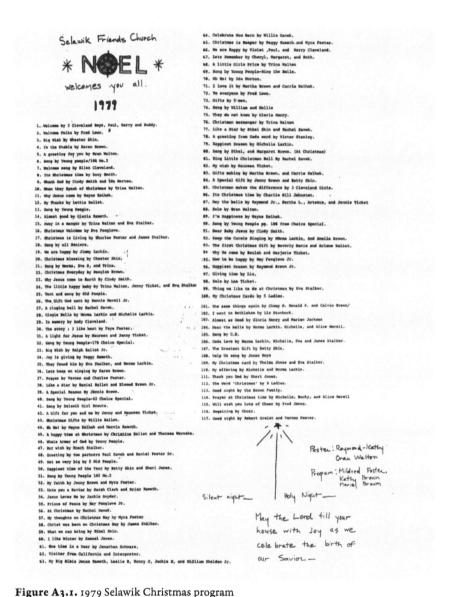

Figure A3.1. 1979 Selawik Christmas program

https://doi.org/10.5876/9781646426065.c013

References

Anderson, Douglas D. 1988. *Onion Portage: The Archaeology of a Stratified Site from the Kobuk River, Northwest Alaska*. Anthropological Papers of the University of Alaska 22(1–2). Fairbanks.

Anderson, Douglas D. 2023. *The Inupiat of Northwest Alaska over the Past Millennium*. Tuscaloosa: Borgo Publishing.

Anderson, Douglas D., and Wanni W. Anderson. 1968–1982. Field notes, Selawik, Alaska. 12 vols. In possession of the authors.

Anderson, Douglas D., and Wanni W. Anderson. 1970. *An Anthropological Survey of the Selawik Drainage*. Report submitted to the US National Park Service.

Anderson, Douglas D., and Wanni W. Anderson.1977. *Prehistoric and Early Historic Human Settlements and Resource Use Areas in the Selawik Drainage, Alaska. Final Report (Part 1) to the US National Park Service (CX-9000-6-0111)*. Washington, DC.

Anderson, Douglas D., and Wanni W. Anderson. 2019. *Life at Swift Water Place: Northwest Alaska at the Threshold of European Contact*. Fairbanks: University of Alaska Press.

Anderson, Douglas D., Ray Bane, Richard K. Nelson, Wanni W. Anderson, and Nita Sheldon. 1977. *Kuuvaṅmiut Subsistence: Traditional Eskimo Life in the Latter Twentieth Century*. Washington, DC: US National Park Service.

Anderson, Douglas D., Wanni W. Anderson, Ray Bane, Richard K. Nelson, and Nita Sheldon Towarak. 1998. *Kuuvaṅmiut Subsistence: Traditional Eskimo Life in the Latter*

https://doi.org/10.5876/9781646426065.c014

Twentieth Century. Kotzebue: US National Park Service and Northwest Arctic Borough School District.

Anderson, Wanni W. 2005. *The Dall Sheep Dinner Guest: Iñupiaq Narratives of Northwest Alaska.* Fairbanks: University of Alaska Press.

Anderson, Wanni W., and Ruthie Tatqaviñ Sampson. 2003. *Folktales of the Riverine and Coastal Iñupiat: Unipchallu Uqaaqtuallu Kuunmiuninlu Tagiugmiuninlu.* Kotzebue and Washington, DC: Northwest Arctic Borough School District and the National Endowment for the Humanities.

Barnhardt, Carol. 2001. "A History of Schooling for Alaska Native People." *Journal of American Indian Education* 40 (1): 1–30.

Basso, Keith H. 1996. "Wisdom Sits in Places: Notes on a Western Apache Landscape." In *Senses of Place*, edited by Steven Feld and Keith H. Basso, 53–90. Santa Fe: School for American Research Press.

California Yearly Meeting (California Friends). 1897–1955. Annual Reports and Diaries of the Missions for the Friends Church of California, Pasadena.

Casey, Edward S. 1996. "How to Get from Space to Place in a Fairly Short Stretch of Time: Phenomenological Prolegomena." In *Senses of Place*, edited by Steven Feld and Keith H. Basso, 13–52. Santa Fe: School for American Research Press.

Feld, Steven, and Keith H. Basso. 1996. *Senses of Place.* Santa Fe: School for American Research Press.

Ferguson Store Ledgers. 1940–1951. Unpublished papers in possession of the authors.

Giddings, J. Louis. 1967. *Ancient Men of the Arctic.* New York: Knopf.

Grinnell, Joseph. 1901. *Gold Hunting in Alaska.* Edited by Elizabeth Grinnell. Elgin: David C. Cook.

Hirshberg, Diane, and Suzanne Sharp. 2005. *Thirty Years Later: The Long-Term Effect of Boarding Schools on Alaska Natives and Their Communities.* Report of the Institute of Social and Economic Research, University of Alaska Anchorage.

Jacobsen, Johan Adrian. (1884) 1977. *Alaska Voyage 1881–1883: An Expedition to the Northwest Coast of America, from the German text of Adrian Woldt.* Translated by Erna Gunther. Chicago: University of Chicago Press.

Jenness, Diamond. 1962. "Eskimo Administration: I. Alaska." *Arctic Institute of North America Technical Paper* 10.

Jorgensen, Joseph G. 1990. *Oil Age Eskimos.* Berkeley: University of California Press.

Larsen, Helge. 1968. *Trail Creek: Final Report on the Excavation of Two Caves on Seward Peninsula, Alaska.* Copenhagen: Ejnar Munksgaard.

Lee, Linda, Ruthie Sampson, and Ed Tennant. 1989. *Lore of the Iñupiat: The Elders Speak,* Vol. 1. Kotzebue: Northwest Arctic Borough School District.

Lee, Linda, Ruthie Sampson, and Ed Tennant. 1991. *Qayaqtauginnaqtuaq (Qayaq: The Magical Traveler)*. Kotzebue: Northwest Arctic Borough School District.

Lee, Linda, Ruthie Sampson, and Ed Tennant. 1992. *Lore of the Iñupiat: The Elders Speak*, Vol. 3. Kotzebue: Northwest Arctic Borough School District.

Lee, Linda, Ruthie Sampson, Ed Tennant, and Hannah Mendenhall. 1990. *Lore of the Iñupiat: The Elders Speak*, Vol. 2. Kotzebue: Northwest Arctic Borough School District.

Loon, Hanna, Angeline Newlin, and Ruth Ramoth Sampson, trans. 1979–1980. *Unipchaallu Uqaaqtuallu: Legends and Stories*, Vols. 1 and 2. Anchorage: National Bilingual Materials Development Center, University of Alaska, Anchorage.

Madison, Curt, and Yvonne Yarber. 1981. *Madeline Solomon, Koyukuk: A Biography*. Blaine: Hancock House Publishers.

Michael, Henry, ed. 1967. *Lieutenant Zagoskin's Travels in Russian America, 1842–44*. Arctic Institute of North America, Anthropology of the North, Translations from Russian Sources, No. 7. Toronto: University of Toronto Press.

Oakley, Cochran. 2001. "The Gift of the Child: Iñupiat School Thrives on Love." *Nunatsiaq News*, February 13.

Olsen, Dean F. 1969. *Alaska Reindeer Herdsmen: A Study of Native Management in Transition*. SEG Report No. 18, Institute of Social, Economic and Government Research, University of Alaska, Fairbanks.

Postell, Alice. 1990. *Where Did the Reindeer Come From? Alaska Experience, the First Fifty Years*. Portland: Amaknak Press.

Roberts, Arthur O. 1978. *Tomorrow Is Growing Old: Stories of the Quakers in Alaska*. Newberg, OR: The Barclay Press.

Rotman's Store (Selawik, Alaska). 1940–1942. Ledgers. Documents in possession of Wanni Anderson, Haffenreffer Museum of Anthropology, Brown University, Bristol, Rhode Island.

Said, Edward W. 1994. *Culture and Imperialism*. New York: Vintage Books.

Samms, Carrie. 1898. Diary of 1897 and 1898. Archives, California Society of Friends, Pasadena.

Schneider, William, compiler. 1989. *The Life I've Been Living: Moses Cruikshank*. Fairbanks: University of Alaska Press.

Selawik Friends Church Archives. Selawik, AK.

Simpson, John. 1852. *Journal of Mr. John Simpson, Surgeon of Her Majesty's Ship "Plover," in Command of a Detached Party to the Eastern Head of Hotham's Inlet, Kotzebue Sound, in May 1850. Further Correspondence and Proceedings Connected with the Arctic Expedition, Presented to Both Houses of Parliament Command of Her Majesty*. London.

Skoog, Ronald O. 1968. "Ecology of the Caribou (*Rangifer tarandus granti*) in Alaska." PhD dissertation, Department of Zoology, University of California, Berkeley.

Stern, Richard O., Edward L. Arobio, Larry L. Naylor, and Wayne C. Thomas. 1980. *Eskimos, Reindeer, and Land*. Fairbanks: Agricultural Experiment Station, School of Agriculture and Land Resources Management, University of Alaska, Fairbanks.

Stoney, George M. 1900. *Naval Explorations in Alaska. (US Naval Institute Proceedings of September and December 1899)*. Washington, DC.

Sun, Susan, Florence Douglas, Minnie Gray, Hanna Loon, Angeline Newlin, Ruth Ramoth Sampson, and Bertha Sheldon. 1979. *Kaniosisautit Uqayusragnikun* (Kobuk Inupiat Junior Dictionary). Anchorage: National Bilingual Materials Development Center, Rural Education, University of Alaska, Anchorage.

United States Bureau of Education. 1908. *Annual Report on Introduction of Domestic Reindeer into Alaska, 1891–1908*. Washington, DC: Government Printing Office.

United States Bureau of Education. 1908–1919. Annual Reports to the Commissioner of Education. The National Archives RG No. 75. Washington, DC.

United States Bureau of Education, Alaska Division. N.d. General Correspondence, Letters Received. The National Archives RG No. 75. Washington, DC.

VanStone, James W., John A. Kakaru, and Charles V. Lucier. 2000. "Reindeer Fairs on Seward Peninsula, 1915–1919." *Arctic Anthropology* 37 (2): 60–77.

Index